Billion Dollar Agent Manifesto

Secrets to Grow Your Business to Over $1,000,000

Best Agent Business

and

Steve Kantor

Billion Dollar Agent Manifesto

Secrets to Grow Your Business to Over $1,000,000

Copyright 2013 by Best Agent Business and Steve Kantor

Edited by Jennifer Young and Raquel Martin
Published by Best Agent Business
www.BestAgentBusiness.com

All rights reserved.

No part of this publication may be reproduced or transmitted in any form or by any means, electronic or mechanical, including photocopy, recording or information storage and retrieval methods now known or to be invented, without the written permission of the publisher, except by a reviewer who wishes to quote brief passages in connection with a review written for inclusion in an educational publication, radio, or TV broadcast.

Printed in the United States of America.

2nd Edition – November 2013

ISBN 978-0-9788854-8-9

Please contact Best Agent Business with questions, comments, requests for help, or speaking engagements.

www.BestAgentBusiness.com

Sales@BestAgentBusiness.com

202-297-2393

Table of Contents

Best Agent Business

Client Testimonials

Best Agent Business provides part-time virtual assistant and calling services to top agents. We help you focus on your unique talent and delegate everything else to grow your business.

"Best Agent Business uses a very organized and systematic approach to help real estate agents become top listers. They have a great team approach with fantastic communication and follow-up."

"Three years ago, I was searching for a more efficient and profitable way to run my business. I came across Billion Dollar Agent - a book written by Best Agent Business - read it at least three times and made notes as to what the industry-leading Realtors were doing successfully.

Best Agent preaches systems, processes and follow-up, and has proven year after year that they practice what they preach. After three years of following up with me through email and personal contact, I became their client for life. The lifeblood of my business is being consistent, giving all my customers and clients 100% excellent service so that referrals come effortlessly and consistently.

As a Broker and Owner of an EXIT Realty franchise, I am able to maintain sales volume with little effort and dominate in other important areas including: recruiting, training and servicing other clients and my agents. I plan to use Best Agent Business for my Brokerage to help all my agents succeed in their business. I would recommend Best Agent Business to anyone who is serious about their business."

Introduction

A manifesto is a declaration of the thoughts and beliefs of an individual or a group. It can be a statement of what they intend to do in the future, what they did in the past, and the reasoning behind those actions.

Dedication

I dedicate this book to the real estate agents who see things differently. They imagine. They create. They inspire.

I dedicate this book to the people who encouraged me and my dreams over the past few years. I greatly appreciate your positive influence on my life.

I dedicate this book to the Ishidos at Lifebushido and Best Agent Business who have created something from nothing and are now sharing their knowledge with more people.

I dedicate this book to our clients at Best Agent Business who have worked with us to mutually focus our unique talents in business and in life.

I dedicate this book to everyone who is a current or future Billion Dollar Agent.

I dedicate this book to the rookies of real estate who read this book to be inspired to become a Billion Dollar Agent. Go for it!

I dedicate this book to you, the reader. Read carefully. Read between the lines. Listen deeply. There is something happening.

History

I will share the history of Billion Dollar Agent, Best Agent Business and Lifebushido.

How did we get here? Let me give you a short history leading up to *Billion Dollar Agent Manifesto*.

I grew up in San Diego, went to Harvard for college and graduated in three years. I came to Washington, DC, bought an Apple II plus computer and learned how to program. In my first job out of college, I did economic consulting for Clients such as the CIA, World Bank, IMF and the State Department. I only had one job out of college before starting my own business.

I got a masters from John Hopkins School of Advanced International Studies (SAIS) in Global Theory and History. After graduation, I backpacked around the world for a year and visited over 50 countries. When I returned, I started a software company named Gnossos Software.

Gnossos Software was a database CRM software product company. I like databases. I grew Gnossos Software to a few million in revenue and sold the company in 2004.

I took a year off in 2005 and came up with 100 business ideas. In 2006, I started a few of them under the name Lifebushido. Lifebushido is focused on building a global network of people, working part-time from home, with flexible hours, using their unique talents. We have business, creative and social entrepreneurial ventures. We are global and 100 percent virtual. We have more than 100 staff members who all work part-time and refer to themselves as Ishidos. Our fantastic team provides part-time, virtual assistant and calling services to small business entrepreneurs with $100,000 to $10M in revenue per year.

Best Agent Business is the primary revenue and funding source for Lifebushido ventures. Best Agent Business provides services to top real estate agents. Our target market is agents above $100,000 in GCI. In 2006, when I started Best Agent Business, I realized that out of 1,000,000 real estate agents, probably only a few hundred had sold over $1B in real estate in their career. We started to track down those people. I reached out and interviewed over 70 top agents and coaches and we published *Billion Dollar Agent – Lessons Learned.*

Billion Dollar Agent was well-received by top agents and we continued to do research, and fund the research, with revenue from Best Agent Business. In short, Best Agent Business tests the business model theories from *Billion Dollar Agent.* It all works together smoothly.

In the five years since publishing *Billion Dollar Agent - Lessons Learned,* we have conducted interviews with over 1,000 agents, completed over $1,000,000 worth of customer-driven research, built our Billion Dollar Agent Team to over 100 part-time assistants and callers from over 5,000 job applicants and worked with over 100 top agents as clients of Best Agent Business.

We have over 1,000 pages of solid systems that we use to run Database Management, Lead Management, Marketing, Listing Management, Closing Management, Accounting, Calling, Agent Management, Agent Recruiting and Life Management teams.

As Best Agent Business has grown, I have had over 1,000 30-minute phone call sessions with top agents doing over $100,000 in GCI. Detailed notes have been made during every single call. These notes have been fed back into our knowledge base and systems. We map out the patterns we see across different segments of the industry.

Given the real estate crash in recent years, we delayed the next edition of *Billion Dollar Agent* because it would have been distorted by the crash, surge in REO and short sale business.

For *Billion Dollar Agent Manifesto,* we decided to focus on agents doing more than $1,000,000 in GCI per year. We estimate this number to be less than 1,000 across the country or one in 1,000 agents. Since $1M in GCI is roughly $40 million in sales volume, someone doing those numbers for 20 to 30 years will get to one billion in closed sales volume for their career.

Billion Dollar Agent is like Switzerland. We are independent.

- We are not biased by a geographic area
- We are not biased by doing business at low or high price points
- We are not biased by a REO or short sale focus
- We are not biased by association with one franchise
- We are not biased by association with one coach
- We are not biased by association with one database or one buyer web lead system

Secret Code if you are Currently a Billion Dollar Agent

Lifebushido, Best Agent Business and Billion Dollar Agent are an evolving vision and secret plan, except for those who can read between the lines. Can you read between the lines? Are you currently a Billion Dollar Agent who earned over $1,000,000 in GCI last year? Do you plan to grow to become a Billion Dollar Agent in the next 1,000 days? If so, you should contact us immediately!

There are over 1,000,000 real estate agents in the USA and Canada. We estimate that there are about 1,000 agents who are a Billion Dollar Agent. We are tracking down every single one of them. The following section is for the one in 1,000 agents who are Billion Dollar Agents.

Questions

- Are you happy with your work mix and the percent of your work week that you spend focusing on your unique talents?

- What would happen if you spent 80 percent of your time focusing on your unique talents?

- Are you fine with your current revenue/GCI or do you still want to grow? What is your current GCI and what is your long-term GCI goal?

- Is your net profit only 20 to 40 percent? Do you want to improve your net profit to over 50 percent?

Finances

- What is the current net profit of your business? Do you think that is low, average or high compared to other Billion Dollar Agents? How much do you want to improve your net profit to 50 percent?

- How big can your business grow? What is your Billion Dollar Agent Goal for revenue and GCI in the next 1,000 days? What are your goals for three years from now?

- What is your financial exit strategy and how many years away is it? Are you doing anything creative to shift your personal income to capital gains over the next five to ten years? This means a shift from a 40 percent or higher tax rate to 20 percent.

What if?

What if 100 of the smartest, sharpest and most ambitious real estate team leaders decided to become Billion Dollar Agents and work together to achieve their goals?

What if knowledge was shared freely?

What if each Billion Dollar Agent spent one hour per week sharing their unique talents with other Billion Dollar Agents?

What if there was a structured, organized sequence of steps based on the profile of a Billion Dollar Agent.

What if you were organized into a Billion Dollar Agent Triangle with three fellow BDAs for peer-to-peer mentoring and accountability? What if your group competed against other BDA Triangles to keep the juices flowing?

What if the goal was continuous, incremental improvement? What if everyone agreed to not impulsively try the next thing that comes along?

What if everyone realized that ideas and knowledge are free? Did you know that only the systematic implementation of ideas has value and generates profits?

What if you could focus on your best systems, improve them and share them with other Billion Dollar Agents?

What if you could acquire, plug-and-play the best practices and systems for farm marketing, FSBO and showing to improve your business?

What is the value of increasing the net profit of 100 businesses with revenue of $1,000,000 and net profits of 30 percent to revenue levels of $2,000,000 and net profits of 50 percent?

How fun would it be to work together with peers and collaborate closely with 100 Billion Dollar Agents who you admire and respect?

How pumped up would you be if you could spend one hour per day helping 100 other agents grow their revenue and profits? What if you knew those 100 other agents were spending the same time working to grow your revenue and profits?

Anything is possible…

Letter to Billion Dollar Agents

Dear Billion Dollar Agent,

Congratulations! Your business is off to a great start and you achieved over $1,000,000 in GCI in your most recent year. Very few real estate businesses reach over $1,000,000 revenue. In fact, out of over 1,000,000 real estate agents, less than 1,000 agents have created a team doing over $1M in GCI. You are a one in 1,000 real estate agent! Where can you go from here? I would like you think about three things:

- How will you go from your current level to $10M in GCI or 1,000 deals per year?
- What is your unique talent?
- Which three profit pillars of your business are weak or missing?

How can you grow to $10M in GCI or 1,000 deals?

If you want to grow your business to $10M in GCI or 1,000 deals, you need to get creative. You need to think out-of-the-box. You need to leverage more than you have ever imagined. You need to believe that anything is possible.

Many of you are between $1M to $2M in GCI. Only a few of you are over $2M in GCI. How can you grow your business and team to either $10M GCI or 1,000 deals? There are a few agents who are already doing over 1,000 deals per year. The question is how did they get there?

Choose a Billion Dollar Agent Goal (BDAG) to focus on. If you are in a low price market, such as $100,000/year, then we will have you target 1,000 deals per year which may be $3M in GCI. If your market is $800,000 and your average commission check is $20,000, then you only need 500 deals to achieve $10,000,000 in GCI.

How big is your market area? What is an achievable market share of the total GCI in your area? It should be at least 10 percent and I think that 20 percent is possible. RE/MAX has used a term called Premier Market Presence. This can be defined as achieving a target market share, such as 20 percent, or having the largest market share in the area. There are many Billion Dollar Agents who have achieved a 10, 20, or even 30 percent market share of their area.

Now you have a sense of the total market area and a target goal for your business. Brainstorm all the ways you could grow to that level. I suggest you think through all of the market segments for seller and buyer business and analyze where you stand today. What is possible in future?

What is your unique talent among all the Billion Dollar Agents?

The good thing is everyone is good at many things. The bad thing is that most of you are still trying to do too many things. Do less. Subtract things from your schedule, do nothing and focus.

Imagine that you were being interviewed by a Billion Dollar Agent for a job running part of their business. What is your unique talent? What are you the best at doing? Here are a few possible areas:

- Client Marketing
- Expired Marketing
- FSBO Marketing
- Buyer Open House
- Buyer Web Leads
- Buyer Sign Calls
- Investors
- First-time Home Buyers
- Farm Marketing

- Luxury Marketing
- Calling of Leads
- Sales Management of Buyer's Agents
- Systems
- Marketing Lead Generation Systems
- Financials to maximize Net Profit

I am sure you can think of a few more. Ask your fellow BDA Agents. Ask your peer agents in your city. Ask your staff. See what other people say. Narrow your list to three choices. Write a paragraph about each of your talents. Zoom in on which you think is the most powerful.

Here is the important part. How many hours per week do you currently spend on that unique talent? During your work week, how many hours do you spend using or improving that unique talent? My guess is that it is only two to ten hours per week. What would happen if you spent 50 percent of your time using that unique talent?

Which three profit pillars of your business are weak or missing?

Every business has a mix of revenue and profit pillars. We want you to focus on the profit pillars with the highest profit margins. For example, a client/SOI seller lead is more profitable than a buyer web lead for a typical team.

What three profit pillars in your business are weak? What core parts of your business could be improved dramatically with the proper focus and unique talents? Estimate your current GCI per year and the possible GCI per year. What is the gap? Which revenue pillars are totally missing and which ones have the most potential?

For example, maybe you used to work expireds in your early years, you were successful, but now you are not working expireds. Maybe you know that farm marketing would be useful, but you have not gotten that going. Perhaps you know that many BDAs are closing

$100,000 to $200,000 in GCI per year from buyer web business. You never started that revenue pillar and you still get only 50 leads per month from buyer web leads. What is the potential GCI of these missing revenue pillars?

Review the list of weak or missing revenue pillars and narrow it down to the top three based on the potential revenue upside. Do not analyze the pillars by whether you have the time or skill to implement them. We will help you focus on your unique talent and delegate everything else.

Summary

You now have an idea of what is holding you back from $10M or 1,000 deals. You analyzed the total market size to see what is possible in a few years. You identified your unique talent and calculated how many hours per week you could spend using that unique talent. Most importantly, you are focused on the three revenue pillars you need and to move towards your BDAG. Share that BDAG with me and your fellow BDAs. I will help you make it happen.

Introduction

Best Agent Business

Client Testimonials

Best Agent Business provides part-time virtual assistant and calling services to top agents. We help you focus on your unique talent and delegate everything else to grow your business.

"Best Agent Business has been great at taking all the lower-priced items off my plate and I know they are getting done! They have allowed me to focus on the higher dollar tasks and take much-needed time to spend with family. Hands down, this has been the best decision dollar-for-dollar that I have spent to make my business efficient! Thanks so much! I am looking for more activities to hand over so I can continue to leverage my business."

"As a mega-producing agent, implementing and maintaining systems is a key priority. Best Agent Business took my business to the next level by helping me get organized and focused on the right things. Steve's staff is professional, dependable and experienced. They will help you make more money now!"

Focus Unique Talents

Focus on Unique talents

I will discover and focus on my unique talent during focus hours.

The key to becoming a Billion Dollar Agent is focus. You must focus more than other agents and teams. You must discover your unique talent and spend increasing amounts of time on your unique talent. You must use the Time Management System of a Billion Dollar Agent and schedule focus hours. You must slow down to focus more. In 100 days, the average real estate agent doing over $100,000 in GCI can instantly become twice as productive with their time using our time management system.

Focus

The secret to becoming a Billion Dollar Agent is focus. Focus on your unique talent and delegate everything else. Steve Jobs focused. Concert violinists focus. Olympic athletes focus. Focus means success. Focus is a deep connection forged with a first-time buyer during a buyer consultation. Focus is helping a seller price their home properly to sell it within 30 days. Focus is spending a focus hour calling your buyer/seller leads without touching email. Focus is a weekly strategy hour to work ON your business. Focus is not easy.

The human brain is built to allow and adapt to distraction and interruption. Being in a state of flow and focus is hard. This is why so few small business entrepreneurs are able to achieve even $1M in revenue. Focus is hard. Focus is difficult. Focus is not natural, not easy and not a typical skill of a top agent.

What is the main difference between a $200,000 agent and a $1,000,000 agent? The answer is focus. You increase your focus one day at a time. You can develop daily habits and rituals, in ten days, using our Perfect Day and Time Management systems.

Once you establish your daily habits and rituals, we can place you in a Billion Dollar Agent Triangle with two other top agents. The triangle will do a daily email for 100 days that will transform your sense of time management and your ability to focus. Habits are not formed in 21 days. Habits are formed over 100 days.

The amount of time you waste every single day is huge. Right now, more than 50 percent of your time is wasted by doing nothing. You drive around in cars doing nothing, you lose focus or you do $20/hour tasks which should be delegated ASAP. How many hours a week are you truly engaged in focus hours? What would happen if you instantly doubled those focus hours daily?

Leverage

All successful businesspeople understand the power of leverage. Solid time management is simply achieving leverage over the 40 to 60 hours per week of work you are currently spending on your business. Time management is a missing ingredient for almost all top agents. Best Agent Business has created and tested our time management system with over 100 agents over the past few years.

With our time management system, you can leverage your time and be twice as productive within 100 days. At the end of the 100 days, you will be happier with your work and business, get along better with your family and staff, have less stress in your life and be working fewer hours.

Unique Talent

Everyone has a unique talent. Many people have a few unique talents.

- What do you love to do in real estate?
- What pumps you up and gives you positive emotional energy?
- What do you do best or better than almost anyone else you know in real estate?

- What do you do that makes time slow down and disappear and you are in a state of flow?
- What do you look forward to on your daily schedule?

Real Estate has Hundreds of Tasks

A real estate agent who works alone is responsible for doing a few hundred different types of tasks every single week. This is the worst possible arrangement for a business and a key reason why most real estate agents are constantly stressed, multi-tasking and failing to get anything done. In fact, the average full-time real estate agent who should be working 2,000 hours per year only works about 20 percent or 400 hours per year. What are they doing the other 80 percent of the time?

When you start a business, you do pretty much everything to start. The faster you delegate and the fewer things you do, the faster you will grow. The more you grow, the more money you will make and the happier you will be.

Time Spent on Unique Talent

In a typical work week, what percent of your time do you spend on your unique talent? Is it ten, 20, 40, 60 or 80 percent? For example, if you work 40 hours per week and spend eight hours on your unique talent, that would be 20 percent. Write down your number.

What would happen to your business if you could double the hours you spend on your unique talent? Do you have control over the hours you spend on your unique talent or do you not have control? The answer is easy. You have 100 percent control over the time you spend on your unique talent. If you disagree, call me and I can prove it.

If you doubled the hours spent on your unique talent over the next 100 days, you could increase your net profit by 50 to 100 percent over the next year. That is a powerful statistic.

Example of Unique Talent Activities for Real Estate

You may be having a difficult time deciding what your unique talents are. Here are just a few examples to get your mind working:

Meeting

- Listing appointment with a regular seller
- Listing appointment with a FSBO or expired
- Showing buyers potential homes
- Buyer consultation
- Visiting your buyer client at their new house
- Attending a client closing
- Meeting a Client-A or SOI-A who has given you referrals
- Meeting a Vendor-B who may give you referrals
- Meeting with a networking group

Calling

- Scheduled 15 minute seller consultation
- Scheduled 15 minute buyer consultation
- First phone call to a buyer or seller lead
- Calling clients
- Calling SOI
- Calling seller leads
- Calling buyer leads

When – Where – Who

When is the best time for you to focus on your unique talent? Is it in the early morning before anyone else is awake in the house? Is it regular mornings from 8 a.m. to 10 a.m. or 9 a.m. to 11 a.m.? Is it in the afternoons? Which day of the week or days of the week? Each unique talent will ultimately have an ideal time of day and days of the week which is the best fit for you. Where is the best place to do that unique talent? Think about the best possible location.

Who are you with when you do that unique talent? Some unique talents are done by you, solo, without anyone else. Some are done with one other person. Some are done with a few other people. Decide what your unique talent is and pick the best possible place, time and company for you to focus on that talent.

Priority of Unique Talent Activities

How do you organize and decide what type of unique talent activities to do? At first, you may think that it would be best to spend 100 percent of your time on unique talents. That is close to impossible, but I think an ultimate goal of 80 percent is possible for a true Billion Dollar Agent who is growing from $1M to $5M in GCI or more.

You have 100 percent control over some unique talents and you can create something from nothing overnight. Others, such as listing appointments with sellers, are dependent on other aspects of business flow. Here is how you should organize your focus hours for unique talent slots:

- **A** - These are your best unique talent activities, such as listing appointments or meeting for a buyer consultation. You do not have 100 percent control over the quantity of these activities.

- **Backup** - These are second tier backup activities, in case you do not have enough A. For example, if you have a 2:00 p.m. to 4:00 p.m. time slot daily for a listing appointment, and you do not have a listing appointment scheduled for the coming day, you could email or call client/SOI/vendors. Schedule a get together, meet for coffee or use that time slot to do calling of your seller leads.

- **Lead Generation -** This is a bit complex to understand. You can use your focus hour timeslots to do lead generation activities which will generate more unique talent options. For example, you may spend an hour writing ten notes to client/SOI/vendors to touch base. Reach out and suggest you meet for coffee/lunch and ask them to call you. If you send ten notes, you have a positive touch with those ten people and the two to three who respond will fill a future focus hour.

Personality Profile – Calm Cathy – Hyper Harry – Rockstar Rick

I will aspire to increase my Rockstar Rick personality traits and control my Hyper Harry impulses.

The most likely personality to become a Billion Dollar Agent is a Rockstar Rick. A Rockstar Rick is an emerging businessperson, rather than a salesperson only, who has long-term goals to grow to over $1,000,000 in GCI with solid profits. Rockstar Ricks are usually at $100,000 to $1,000,000 in GCI and the majority are at $300,000 and above. There are many top agents who are a combination of Hyper Harry and Rockstar Rick profiles. The more you manage the Hyper Harry side and become more like a Rockstar Rick, the more successful you will be.

Personality Profiles

Just like a DISC or Myers-Briggs personality profile test, we have created a simple grouping of agents:

- Slow Sally
- Calm Cathy
- Hyper Harry
- Rockstar Rick
- Billion Dollar Agent Brandy

Often, agents can correctly self-identify their own profile. At Best Agent Business, we do not work with Slow Sallys – those are the 80 percent of agents who do less than $50,000 per year.

Who is Rockstar Rick?

A Rockstar Rick is a top agent who already has had solid success and passionately aspires to grow their business and become a Billion Dollar Agent Brandy. If you are fine with staying at $300,000 and not growing to $1,000,000, then you are a Calm Cathy, not a Rockstar Rick.

We identify a Rockstar Rick by these traits:

- **Mental State** – Calm with focus and energy for growth
- **Focus** – Solid time management with constant delegation
- **Financial Management** – Monthly financials with net profit goals

Mental State

Rockstar Ricks always have positive attitudes. They are optimistic and exude optimism with their self-talk, their staff, and their clients. They have a strong personality, not weak or average. They are more likely to be calm than hyper. At times they will get very passionate and energized about certain topics. This natural hypomania moves them forward towards their Billion Dollar Agent Goal.

In the face of adversity, Rockstar Ricks are emotionally resilient. They have 'grit'. They persevere. When a deal crashes and burns, they immediately focus on the solution rather than getting angry, mad, upset or sad. While other Slow Sallys and Hyper Harrys go off the deep end in sadness, anger, or regret, the Rockstar Rick solves the problem and moves on to close the same deal in the future.

Rather than being an extreme extrovert like Hyper Harry, or more of an introvert like a Calm Cathy, a Rockstar Rick is an ambivert, which is a mixture of both traits. Sales studies have shown that ambiverts outperform extroverts. The basic traits are an ability to listen and talk. Hyper Harrys are pure high I extroverts. This leads to tons of business from sheer charisma, high energy and enthusiasm. I can point you to many Rockstar Ricks with fewer leads and fewer clients/SOI/friends who are doing far more net profit than the Hyper Harrys next door.

Rockstar Ricks like to work at a solid pace, not too fast and not too slow. They like routine. The more routine things are, the better they do. Rockstar Ricks usually work less hours than Hyper Harrys or Calm Cathys because they have excellent time and life management skills.

Focus on Time Management

If you look at the schedules/calendars of Rockstar Ricks for the coming week, it is likely that they have 50 to 80 percent of their time already scheduled. This is because they have a perfect day and have solid time blocks for focus, buffer and free time. They practice our Billion Dollar Agent Time Management System and Kaizen weekly to tune their perfect day to a perfect fit.

Hyper Harrys run around like chickens with their heads cut off and they waste at least 20 to 30 percent of their working hours. Rockstar Ricks are always on time. They start on time, they end on time. They are punctual.

Financial Management

Most salespeople hate accounting. Most small businesspeople are bad at accounting. Most entrepreneurs do not like accounting. Rockstar Ricks are emergent businesspersons. They focus on the following:

- Profits not transactions
- Monthly accounting rather than a shoebox of receipts
- Separate business accounts instead of mixed finances
- Planned spending not impulsive purchases
- Spends 10 percent on marketing instead of wasting 20 percent
- Profit not ego
- Making a profit instead of crushing it

A Rockstar Rick above $200,000 in GCI has a Billion Dollar Agent Goal, a BDAG, of over $1,000,000 in GCI with a net profit of 50 percent or $500,000 within 1,000 days.

Billion Dollar Agent Brandy

Here is a sneak peek at the highest Billion Dollar Agent level:

- Over $1,000,000 in GCI
- Open to sharing financials with other top agents
- Monthly progression toward profit goals
- No ego
- Focus on helping others

Warning for Hyper Harry

If you are a Hyper Harry or a combination of Hyper Harry and Rockstar Rick, here are some concerns and thoughts:

- Impulsive actions such as starting and stopping relationships with vendors can hurt you and your business.

- Buying shiny objects, such as more leads, almost always reduces your net profit.

- There is no magic button or secret.

- There are many people who will try to take advantage of you and leverage your Hyper Harry personality to put you in a situation where you impulsively buy their magic button.

- Having a set number of deals as your focus and goal will almost always lead you down the road to lower profits.

- If you continue to be a Hyper Harry, you may grow from $200,000 to $500,000 in GCI over the next 1,000 days, but sooner or later you will read this book or speak to a Billion Dollar Agent Brandy. You will realize you need to get help to complement your Hyper Harry talents.

Summary

Who are you? Are you a Calm Cathy, Hyper Harry, or Rockstar Rick? How can we help you?

Meet, Call, or Other

I will meet more people, call more people and schedule more meetings.

You only do three things at work – meet, call or other. You are meeting with people, calling outbound leads or doing other stuff. Compare your current schedule with how you want to allocate your time in the future. You need to spend more time meeting people. You need to consistently spend one, two or three hours calling people. You need to spend less time doing other things and focus on delegating.

Let's define what we mean by meet, call and other:

- **Meet** – This includes meeting with people face-to-face whether it is clients, leads, people you know or new people you are meeting for the first-time.

- **Call** – This is outbound calling of seller leads, buyer leads and cold call leads such as expired, FSBO or clients/SOI/vendors. This does not include answering phone calls, talking to buyers at the showing stage, sellers who are listed with you or anyone under contract.

- **Other** – Other includes everything which is not meeting or calling. This may include strategic planning, marketing, planning, delegating, incoming phone calls, talking to agents, talking to clients about deals in process, assistant work, paperwork, surfing the web, driving around the city, zoning out on social media and other things.

Time Management Weekly Analysis

A typical agent who wants to become a future Billion Dollar Agent is currently working 50 hours a week. Let's see how they currently use their time versus the proper future plan.

	Now	Future
Meet	15 hours	25 hours
Call	5 hours	10 hours
Other	30 hours	15 hours
Total Weekly	50 hours	50 hours

In this example, you would simply go from one hour of calling per day to two hours of calling and spend two more hours per day meeting with people. This change alone will likely lead to a 50 percent increase in profits.

Key Focus Lessons

- **Review Shift Weekly** –Sit down every Sunday or Monday; review your calendar for the prior and coming week. How did the week FEEL? Did you have too much of one type of work or too little of another? Shift your schedule every single week. After ten weeks, you will feel like a new person. You will feel like you have enough clarity and dynamic focus to conquer the world. Look at your schedule for the coming week and see if there is anything you can do to positively impact the overall mix for the week.

- **Best Better Good -** For each type of work, there is always a best possible activity, a better and a good option. You have 100 percent control of your Perfect Day and your weekly schedule. If you do not believe this, you will never become a Billion Dollar Agent. You have 100 percent control of your schedule. Start acting like it. If you cannot find work for the best option, go to the better option. If you cannot find better, do good.

- **Calling Generates Meetings -** You can spend one hour of calling to generate four hours of meeting. This is a typical ratio. If you do not like calling your Clients/SOI to touch base, call them to schedule a meeting for coffee or lunch. The way you close deals is by meeting with people. The way you schedule meetings is by calling people. It is great if they respond to your email. If they do not, you need to call them.

Meetings are Not Appointments

We use the word meetings instead of appointments because meetings are more inclusive. Usually, the word appointment refers to a listing appointment or a buyer consultation. Meetings include dropping off a house-warming gift to a client, meeting people at an open house or going to a networking event.

Meeting – Leads Core and New People

There are three types of meetings:

- **Leads** - Meeting with leads is the best possible type of meeting. Imagine you met with one seller or buyer lead every single day. You would close a lot of business.
    - Seller Listing Appointments
    - Buyer Consultations - A buyer consultation is an in-office meeting to review buyer needs, explain the process and get a signed buyer's agreement. The showing agent shows them properties.
    - Buyer Showings - If you are still doing all the buyer business yourself, you are spending five to 20 hours per buyer showing homes. This ultimately is $20/hour work which should be delegated to a showing agent. Most agents think this is one of the most valuable tasks they do when it is really worth only $20/hour. The

proof of this is the thousands of agents who would gladly show property on a part-time basis for $20/hour.

- **Core -** Your core is your database of clients, SOI and vendors. Their core provides top agents with more than 50 percent of their net profit, yet 80 percent of agents undervalue it.

    - Clients – These are the people you have closed business with. Your goal is to revive them, extend rapport and help them generate repeat business and referral leads.

    - SOI – These are the people who have never done a deal with you. Some of them have referred business to you. You want to be sure to get their business when they do their next real estate deal.

    - Vendors - Vendors often provide a large percentage of referrals and are not treated with the proper attention and respect by agents.

- **New People -** You are constantly meeting new people. The best agents always add their information to the database as a new SOI so they can get your monthly email and mailed newsletter. You randomly meet new people while going about your life and networking events.

For each type of meeting, decide the best possible place and time. What days of the week are best for which type of meetings? What is the best location? What is the best time of day? Based on this information, schedule time slots for your perfect day.

Develop a Meeting System

A meeting system is a process used to identify and tag the people in your database you want to meet with, reach out to, invite to meet and follow-up with after a meeting. For example, you may decide to have two meetings per week or 100 meetings per year with your core database. If you have 1,000 clients/SOI/vendors in your core, who are you going to meet with? You should start with your Client-A, SOI-A, and Vendor-A core contacts who have already given you referrals. Meet with the people you enjoy the most to energize your life. Meet with the people you think could lead to multiple referrals based on their business or social situation.

Calling

Calling brings out reality guilt and honesty issues among agents. Everyone knows that salespeople call leads to close sales. Everyone knows that 80 percent of real estate agents are not salespeople and should be fired. You got to where you are now by spending some fraction of your time calling leads. Here are a few ways to solve reality, guilt and honesty issues:

- **Reality -** Face reality. Are their leads to call? Did you include your core in your quarterly calls? Did you remember all the leads from Zillow, Trulia, Realtor.com and other sources you received in the last year that no one has spoken to? On average, how much time are you spending calling over the past 100 days or three months? Are you calling for 30 minutes, one hour or two hours a day? Are you calling consistently without any exceptions? This average amount is your reality. Face reality.

- **Guilt -** Stop feeling guilty about reality. It is what it is. There is no value in feeling guilty. It is better to face reality and act with honesty.

- **Honesty - A** Billion Dollar Agent will spend one, two or three hours calling per day for five days per week. Those are your only three choices. If you are going to call less than one hour per day, you are not cut out to be a Billion Dollar Agent.

You only have three choices…

How many hours per day are you going to do calling? Are you going to call one, two or three hours per day? Make a decision now. This decision is big because it drives the rest of your perfect day schedule. You need to make a commitment and make it happen. If your decision is one to two hours per day, stick with one hour to be conservative. There is no such thing as one to two hours, two to three hours or one and a half hours. The only choices you have are one, two or three hours. Keep life simple.

Here are the types of Calling:

- **Leads -** The best type of lead calling is a scheduled phone consultation with a lead.
    - Scheduled Phone Consultation - You may use an online scheduler to time block 15 to 30- minute seller or buyer phone consultations. In the last few years, I have had over 1,000 scheduled, 30-minute phone consultations with agents making over $100,000 in GCI. I can document every single call, person, date, time and outcome.
    - Scheduled Meeting - This is when you speak to a new seller or buyer lead and convert them to an appointment. You can also speak to a previous BC lead who is now an A lead ready for an appointment.
    - Resolve and Qualify Leads - Often, when you get new leads from signs or the web, you need to reach them live in order to qualify them.
- **Core -** Do you call your core database of clients/SOI/vendors? Does anyone call them? Your core should be called quarterly and connected to monthly mailings, seasonal contests and

client appreciation events. If you have 1,000 people in your core, you should personally call 100 of them. Have your caller reach out to the other 900. This amounts to four dials per year for 900 people. This is 200 to 300 hours of calling or $4,000 to $6,000 worth of work at a rate of $20/hour. That means you will spend approximately $5,000 a year to call 900 people once a quarter. Your caller can say hello, leave a voice message and send an email after the call.

- **New** - Calling new people is similar to cold calling. This would be calling FSBO, expireds or people you want to reach out to.

Other

Other may appear to be too broad of a term, so let's zoom down to specifics. Other is not meeting or calling. Other does not include the time you spend meeting or calling people during the work week.

Other can be Good, Required, or Bad

- Good other time is when Billion Dollar Agents run and grow their business. You cannot spend ALL of your time meeting and calling. You would get burned out and your business would not operate unless you had a COO to run the business for you

- Required other time is time spent doing things you must do because you have not delegated them. You are the only one that can get them done.

- Bad other time is how 80 percent of real estate agents spend 80 percent of their work hours. Bad other time is unproductive, it is hours wasted. It is not how you should spend your time.

Delegate, Do and Drive

Let's examine simple ways to chunk other work:

- **Delegate** - The best possible way to spend other time spent is to delegate tasks. You need to focus on your unique talents and delegate everything else. Your unique talents are probably a combination or meeting and calling. Delegating work includes the use of a strategy hour where you craft strategic plans for your business. You work on marketing, creating, reviewing, approving systems and delegating meeting/calling work to your staff. In a perfect world, a Billion Dollar Agent would spend ALL of their other time delegating tasks.

- **Do** - This is when you are doing work which should be delegated in the future. You may be answering the phone, doing assistant work, doing paperwork, doing accounting work, doing database work, doing listing work or closing work. Almost everything you are doing is $20/hour work.

- **Drive** - The amount of time agents spend driving is far more than most people realize. Hyper Harry Agents pop themselves into a car to make it seem like they are going somewhere or doing something. When you are driving, you are making $0 per hour. Let me repeat that. Driving makes $0 per hour. You should get a courier service or a gopher ASAP. Delegate as much driving as possible. One Billion Dollar Agent actually hired a full-time driver for $30,000/year so they can be in the back seat of the car calling, working or resting as they go about their ten listing appointments every week. They are a very smart Billion Dollar Agent.

Other Scary Stuff – Dwell, Dawdle and Diddle

Imagine all the hundreds of thousands of real estate agents in their offices Monday through Friday from 10 a.m. to 2 p.m. What are they doing? The scary thing is, they are probably not calling anyone. Eighty percent of agents are in this position. They should quit and go find a job paying $25,000 to $40,000 a year. If they are not calling, do you think they are meeting? They are not because they are in the office between 10 a.m. and 2 p.m. They may be meeting with other agents, but that is not what we mean by meeting. They do not have a Perfect Day Plan. They have never heard of a Perfect Day Plan. Here is what I think they are doing:

- **Dwell -** A mind at rest will dwell on stuff. The stuff they dwell on is usually negative, mindless and will not move their lives forward. We have all experienced it. A mind at rest will ramble and dwell on non-helpful things. Mindset is critical for business success. You must proactively manage your mindset or you will dwell in despair. Have you been there? I have been there and I am fairly successful in business. Almost every top coach will emphasize that what goes on between your ears is the most important part of your business. I agree.

- **Dawdle -** If you do not have a plan for your day or good time management, you will dawdle away your day. You walk to the corner to get coffee. You go to the bathroom a few extra times per day. You read the newspaper very slowly in the morning. You watch the morning news and suck down 60 minutes of your day. All of these things amount to $20,000 to $50,000 per year in wasted time. Most agents are doing the daily dawdle from 10 a.m. to 2 p.m.

- **Diddle -** Diddling requires a smartphone and more energy than dawdling. Diddling is poking around on your smartphone checking email, checking social media, or surfing the web. Hyper Harrys have trouble focusing. If they are not meeting or calling people, they often start diddling. Diddlers have a problem with focus. They are addicted to their smartphone, email and social media. They diddle Facebook. They diddle

Twitter. They diddle incoming email. The Internet is designed to encourage you to diddle and eventually to addict you.

Team Colors

I will create a strong team comprised of the right balance of team colors.

A strong Billion Dollar Agent Team is composed of a balance of team colors. You need a proper mix of red, blue, yellow and green. To simplify the widely used DISC personality profile, here is a simple color version:

- **Red -** Driver Entrepreneur - DI on DISC
- **Blue -** Assistant and Systems - CS on DISC
- **Yellow -** Outgoing Meeter and Talker - IS on DISC
- **Green -** Supportive Helper - SC on DISC

To create a Billion Dollar Agent Team, you need to add team colors to your business in the proper sequence and mix so you can focus on your unique talents. If you have too much of one color and not enough of another color, you may become stuck at a certain size of business.

Many team models look at the positions they need to fill in a team. I would like you to think outside the box. Think in terms of colors and how your staff fit into those roles. Here is a way to look at colors via our Billion Dollar Agent model:

- **Red -** Business Owner – You – Focus on your unique talent of spending 80 percent of your time Meeting or Calling people.

- **Blue** – Assistants – This includes both virtual Best Agent Business assistants as well as in-house Assistants (IHAs). It also includes systems which are designed to run your business. You want your business to be more systems-dependent than people-dependent as it grows to over $1,000,000 in GCI.

- **Yellow -** Showing Agents - Showing agents show homes to buyers at an hourly rate. They conduct open houses and network with people around town. They are super-friendly, positive people who love to meet and speak to people. Yellow people are outgoing talkers similar to IS personalities on the DISC personality profile.

- **Green** – Greens are supportive helpers similar to SC personalities on the DISC profile.

Here is a short version of a perfect growth plan:

- You are red and you are so busy you can't keep up with everything.

- You hire blue to delegate assistant work to. Blue creates blue systems in order to prepare for more colors.

- As you get more buyers than you can handle, you hire yellow as showing agents.

- As business grows, you expand your marketing to generate more leads. You get so many new leads, you can't handle them. You hire green as callers so you can stop wasting leads.

Please note carefully that you will now have three important new roles:

- **Systems** - This is not a person; this is how your business operates. This is a Michael Gerber E-Myth basic. You either get it or you do not. This is how your business becomes a business and not self-employment.

- **Showing Agent** - There are plenty of friendly yellow agents who would gladly be a part-time, $20/hour showing agent. The buyer agent model has failed for the majority of teams; they just do not understand it. This concept is critical for a team to transform into the Billion Dollar Agent model.

- **Caller** - You need more calling hours in your business. Your time is limited. If you are above $500,000 in GCI, you should be spending one to two hours a day calling yourself. Your buyer's agents shouldn't be doing any calling. You need enough callers to stop wasting leads. At first, all callers can be virtual such as our Best Agent Business callers. Once you grow above a certain point, it makes sense to have a combination of in-house callers and Best Agent Business callers.

Growing to Become a Billion Dollar Agent

We will describe the path you need to take to transform yourself from a solo agent into a team by adding the proper colors in the proper sequence.

Red

Business owners and small business entrepreneurs are often red. They have the drive to dominate and the ambition to grow their business. The majority of top agents are red.

Strong Points of Red

- Drive
- Energy
- Sales skills
- Sales passion
- Marketing energy to generate more leads
- Passion to grow constantly
- Constantly pushing everything and everyone forward
- Fantastic at converting buyers or sellers on the phone
- Fantastic at in-person listing appointments
- Fantastic at getting buyers to sign agreements in-person

Weak Points of Red

- Lack of an ability to implement systems
- Overly strong personality can offend blue and green people who work for you
- Impatient
- Lacks a warm fuzzy side
- Gradually gets bored with buyers
- Ignores the buyer side of business
- Moves too fast without focus
- Generates more leads than they can work
- Impulsively spends money on new things
- Impulsively stops doing things that work well

The power and drive of a red will help get a new agent to $100,000. They will start to get so busy that there will be more blue assistant work. They will have less time to complete the work and they will begin to avoid it at all costs. For example, a listing animal may start to dread listing appointments because a successful appointment will mean spending two to five hours on blue tasks to process and market the listings.

What color are you? Almost all Billion Dollar Agents are red. Most top agents are red.

You Need Blue

Every agent with over $100,000 in GCI needs a blue, part-time assistant. Based on many models, you should be spending ten percent of your GCI on assistants. Thus, if you are earning $100,000 per year, you should be spending $10,000 per year.

At this level, your time is worth $100/hour if you are doing sales activities but you are spending 50 percent of your time doing $20/hour assistant work. If you hire an assistant for ten to 15 hours per week, you stop doing the $20/hour work and spend more time doing the $100/hour work.

Strong Points of Blue

- Ability to focus
- Attention to detail
- Gets work done
- Gets stuff organized

Weak Points of Blue

- Does not like to meet people
- Does not like to call people
- Does not like change or rapid growth

Systems are blue and they are key to success in business. Without systems, you are a self-employed person with a job. Best Agent Business' systems are the best value we provide to our clients. These systems have been developed with over $1,000,000 in research and development and over 1,000 pages of documentation.

If you are red, and not very good with systems, you need to buy systems that already exist, or hire someone to run your operations and build out systems. If you can get systems work done at the rate of $20/hour, then every moment you spend trying to build systems yourself is not the best use of your red time.

Yellow Showing Agents

I love showing agents. Our vision of the showing agent model has progressed during the last few years to be a key to our Billion Dollar Agent Profit Model. This is a very important concept.

If you are doing $1,000,000 in GCI, our Showing Agent System will deliver an extra $100,000 per year in net profit compared to a regular buyer's agent team model. We are proving the concept. At this point, we are not spending time trying to convince agents to use this model; we are just working with the smartest ten to 20 percent who get it.

Yellow is the friendly person who thought real estate was showing nice people pretty homes and helping them to buy a house. Yellow people are outgoing, talkative and friendly. They are high I. The DISC profile of a Yellow is IS. They are great showing agents but terrible buyer's agent because they will not pick up the phone, make calls, or deal with constant rejection and the boredom of lead follow-up. All they do is make friends quickly. Out of 100 buyer's agents, 80 of them are probably showing agents in the wrong job description.

Yellow does not want to know that real estate involves about 200 different types of tasks including salesperson red stuff, database blue stuff, lead management, systems/assistant work and green stuff like diligently spending two to three hours per day calling leads and making proper database notes for solid follow-ups. Yellow just wants to get out there and be yellow, shine and meet people. Let yellow be yellow!

Our Showing Agent System involves hiring multiple, part-time yellow showing agents on a $20/hour basis. In some markets it may be $15/hour and in others it may be higher. There are no bonuses or commissions. Yellow showing agents making $20/hour will be far happier than buyer's agents who are paid a 50/50 split. You need to trust me on this.

Strong Points of Yellow

- Loves to connect and meet new people
- Bonds and develops rapport fast
- Likes to talk to and learn about people
- Awesome at open houses and showing homes to buyers
- Great at networking at group events

Weak Points of Yellow

- Without focus, yellow would spend most of their time talking with other friendly agents
- Does not like to make consistent follow-up calls
- Will not follow systems unless they are required to as part of job and they are held accountable

Yellow should be hired to help with following:

- Showing homes to buyers
- Licensed work such as inspections and related tasks
- Open houses
- Networking events
- Client appreciation events
- Adding to the SOI database

Green Callers Grow

You need to do more calling. You are likely over spending on marketing and wasting leads. You need more calling hours. It doesn't matter if you spend one, two or three hours calling per day, your business needs more calling. Hiring another three buyer's agents will not help. If you hire three more buyers' agents and they all spend zero hours calling, you would still have zero hours of calling. You need callers.

Strong Points of Green

- Follows systems and likes to help and support people
- Good listener for buyer and seller leads
- Good note taker
- Follow database management systems
- Understands that patience and consistent follow-up is key
- Has a helper/counselor mindset

- Wants to help your business
- Hates to see anyone wasting leads

Weak Points of Green

- Not usually a closer.

Green should be hired to help with following:

- Calling all types of people for your business
- Calling core clients/SOI/vendors to touch base
- Calling buyer leads
- Calling seller BC leads
- Calling expired and FSBO seller leads
- Calling sellers monthly/weekly for seller feedback
- Calling buyers to verify that the showing agent was a good fit and followed systems
- Calling clients during closing management to insure client comfort
- Calling clients after closings to debrief them and ask for referrals

Color Team Balance

A Billion Dollar Agent Team doing $1,000,000 in GCI will have a balance of red, blue, yellow, and green. If you think about a business with 140 deals a year, balanced between buyers and sellers with a $7,000 average commission check, your team should look similar to the following:

- **Red** - One person. This person is you, the business owner.
- **Blue** – You should spend ten percent of your GCI on assistants/systems. This is about $100,000 a year.
- **Yellow** – Spend five percent of your GCI on showing agents. If you have 70 deals at an average of $500 your showing agent fees will be about $50,000 a year.

- **Green** – Spend ten percent of your GCI calling clients/SOI, buyer, and seller leads. This is a budget of $100,000.

Color Sequence Problems

Sometimes people make a mistake and hire colors in the wrong sequence or without balance:

- **Blue and Yellow** - You try to hire one person to do both assistant and showing agent work. It is extremely rare to find someone who is an IC on DISC that is both blue and yellow. Usually, they will do okay with one part of the job and be a failure at the other part. This will hold you back X months until you solve your hiring mistake.

- **Yellow Before Blue** - Never hire a buyer's agent before you hire a blue assistant. Why would you keep doing $20/hour assistant work yourself while you give a commission to a buyer's agent? You need to hire enough blue to get all the assistant work off your plate and develop systems. You need a showing agent in place before you hire your first yellow or leads will get wasted.

- **Marketing Instead of Green** - If you are currently wasting leads, you need more green and callers before you spend more time and money on marketing to generate leads. Marketing is easier, more fun, and generates leads. Lead generation is not the issue anymore. Anyone with money and basic industry knowledge can easily generate 100 leads per month within one to two months. The challenge is lead management, calling the leads and lead conversion. Too often, top agents spend money on marketing before they solve their green gap.

Vacation

I will delegate, and train my team, so I can trust them to run the business without me.

Can your company run without you? Could you go on a vacation for one month and have your company run without you? Do you aspire to build a business that can run and grow without your full-time involvement? What would happen if you travelled for a month with no phone calls and almost no email contact?

I took a one month travel vacation to Israel, India and Istanbul to test the strength of my own business, staff, and systems. I had a fantastic vacation, fully cleared my mind of work and business, spent time with my family, and came back refreshed and recharged.

Here are a few reasons why I decided to take a month off from work to travel:

- **Leave No Regrets -** One of the five secrets of life is having no regrets. I travelled around the world in my youth and had not been on a long trip for many years. I wanted to get out of my comfort zone and travel. I wanted to see India and Israel again. I wanted to go on a long vacation with my wife and have an adventure with my daughter.

- **Clear My Mind -** I work hard and I wanted a long mental break. I watch television and read one to two hours per day, but I hardly did either during the trip.

- **Change My Routine -** At home and work, I have a very structured routine. I wanted to do something different.

- **Delegate -** I worked hard before my trip to delegate more tasks. I noticed there were a number of items that didn't need to flow through me but I had never got them off my plate. It felt good to get them off my plate.

- **Systems -** We have solid systems, but I needed to create a few more so the business could operate smoothly without my involvement.

- **Trust -** I wanted to convey my deep level of trust and confidence in the team I have at Lifebushido and Best Agent Business. Some of my staff may have been worried about my trip, but things worked out fine during my absence.

- **Minimize Communication -** I was able to operate without any phone calls and only 20 emails in 30 days.

- **Grow to the Next Level -** To grow my business, I needed to gradually delegate all possible tasks off my plate and focus on my unique talent. My travels helped me delegate and gain greater clarity on my future focus.

Musings

I sat down about a week after my return and wrote down some personal musings. Some of these related to business and some related to life outside of the business. As a fellow entrepreneur seeking to build a business that can run without your constant presence, I am sure you will relate to many of these:

- The lack of a schedule and structure leads to wandering. That is not healthy, productive or helpful.

- I enjoy sales calls and speaking to people. If there is too little, I miss it. If there is too much, I get burned out. There is an ideal mix of sales calls and meetings.

- Client service issues are depressing, demotivating, and time sucking. They impact salesperson confidence.
- Closing sales does not happen enough without my personal involvement. I need to have systems that will constantly increase the percentage of sales that close without my direct involvement. I also need to constantly reduce the time I spend on closing a sale.
- A client who has been with us for over 100 days and is not ready to provide a written testimonial is a problem. All clients need to be fully engaged and happy by day 100.
- You need to always Kaizen or things fall apart. If you are not improving, your business will fall apart. There needs to be constant Kaizen, constant incremental improvement.
- I dislike dealing with small, operational items which distract and cause stress. Stress is caused by nagging little items I know need to get done. I need to get things off my plate constantly.
- I hate negativity in the morning. I need to wake up at my target of 5:15 a.m. to have peaceful mornings and solid focus.
- Wasteful addictions such as reading a newspaper in the morning, watching TV in the evening, or eating food late at night need to stop.
- After being away for a long time, there are daily habits that may have fallen apart. I need to restart them.

More Random Musings

These musings are random and more personal.

- Meeting with people is the best. I enjoy meeting with new people.

- Never give up.

- The world trip will never end. I spent a year backpacking around the world with two college roommates when we were 25. We called it the world trip.

- Disconnecting from email, work, TV, and reading is a good thing.

- Fear and worry is a waste. Things usually work out. Go with the flow.

- Live life with no regrets.

- Set goals and achieve them.

- Eliminate yourself and delegate faster.

- Everything in the world is the same everywhere.

- I need someone to believe in me. I need pats on the back.

- There is massive global underemployment of college educated global youth. This will grow even more in coming decade.

- Art is for surplus time, cognitive surplus time.

- You can create art or consume art. Most people consume art. Watching TV, listening to music, watching videos on web, surfing web, and reading is consuming art.

- Everyone has addictions. Some are really bad, some are good, and some are neutral or just plain weird.

- I don't like things. I don't like physical objects. I don't like excess.
- I am insanely thankful for and proud of my family.
- Serendipity is something you create for yourself.
- With one success and 100 failures, do you focus on the success or the failures?
- Meditation probably makes sense.
- Focus is everything.
- Life is full of small moments.
- Never give up.

Here are some of the questions and issues I will think about when I return from my travels:

- What questions should I ask myself when I reflect on my month of travel?
- What questions should I ask Ishidos and team leaders?
- What unique talent is missing from the business? What skills or aspects of my talent were missed the most? Basically, what important roles do I have in the company?
- What business systems are the weakest and need improvement?
- Which Ishidos stepped up to the plate or decreased effort/productivity in a negative way?

- What authority was not fully delegated and needs to be delegated in the future?

- Was there any confusion over roles and authority that caused tension? Was there anything that was not resolved or handled fully?

- What else would you need to delegate or improve for you to safely take a one month vacation?

Best Agent Business

Client Testimonials

Best Agent Business provides part-time virtual assistant and calling services to top agents. We help you focus on your unique talent and delegate everything else to grow your business.

"I was doing way too many things, and many of them were not done well. As I delegated items to Best Agent Business one at a time, I began to free up time that allowed me to do more of the things I was good at. I am good at calling, and building relationships. In doing more calling, I gained more referrals. I am leveraging my time and growing the business. Even though I've been in this business for 20 years, my life is more balanced now than it ever was."

"I have been using Best Agent Business for six months. I previously handled all administrative tasks myself, and it was an adjustment to delegate tasks to others. Best Agent Business has saved me time each week and has allowed me to focus more on my clients. I have also become more attuned to my database and have increased contact with my leads."

Delegate Everything Else

Systems

I will create and use systems to constantly improve my business and delegate faster.

When you think about business and delegating, most people think about delegating work to other people. Before you can delegate, you need to create systems. Make a list of the tasks flopping around in your brain. This is the start of a system. This is the first step towards a Billion Dollar Agent business. You need to free up your mind, get your worries out of your head, and make a list of things that need to be done. This will free up your mental energy.

A list becomes a task list. A task list becomes a checklist. Each time you do something, your checklist keeps improving. A checklist might turn into a system a few pages long. When you hire people, they can use your systems and help you create new systems. You can also buy systems already developed by other companies.

If you do not have systems, you are a mess and your business is a mess. You can never grow to become a Billion Dollar Agent. If you have systems, love systems, and find people to create and run systems for you, your business will grow faster.

Delegate Everything Else

The first key to a successful business is to focus on your unique talent. As you spend more time on your unique talent, you will need to delegate and get stuff off your plate.

Every Agent over $100,000 in GCI needs a part-time assistant. Every new real estate agent is the Assistant until they hire an assistant. The majority of real estate agents spend the majority of their time doing assistant work.

A Billion Dollar Agent spends five hours or less per week doing assistant-level work. When we interviewed agents for the first book, most of them said they should have hired their first assistant earlier in their career. They also said that hiring an assistant was one of the most valuable steps they took to delegate everything else.

Why Delegate?

There are three reasons to delegate jobs and a sequence of steps that you should follow:

- **Focus on Your Unique Talent -** You need to spend more time on your unique talent. The only way to do that is to delegate other stuff.

- **New Talents -** You need to delegate important business tasks that are not part of your talent mix. You need to hire other people based on their unique talents. For example, someone else may be better at assistant work, open houses, accounting, or calling buyer web leads.

- **Eliminate Yourself** – The process of starting as a real estate agent to growing to a Billion Dollar Agent is a long process. You need to eliminate the need for your time in the business. You want to be able to take a few weeks of vacation time without freaking out. You want to be able to reduce your hours from 70 hours per week to 50 hours per week. You want to spend five to 20 hours per week on a second business or other community projects. You want to transition into retirement and work fewer hours while still having a business that operates and generates profits without as much of your time.

Delegate to Systems, Services and Staff

You create systems for yourself. You use web software and vendor services to delegate and leverage your time. You start to hire people.

- **Systems -** Paper or computer checklists or documented systems that need to be followed to accomplish business tasks.

- **Services** – Free or paid web and software services such as email, database software, accounting software, and video conferencing used to leverage your time. Vendors provide services such as accountants, virtual assistants, callers, sign companies, stagers, photographers, and others.

- **Staff -** People who are employees or independent contractors working part-time. These people include assistants, showing agents, buyer's agents, couriers, and other people.

If you can find a web service or software that gets something done without people, it is almost always the best approach. If there are vendors that specialize in certain functions and the price is reasonable, it is a far better option than having to recruit, hire, train, fire, and manage on your own.

Systems – Starting Out Alone

At all stages of your business, try to write down the steps you do to perform each activity. Try to focus on tasks that you do daily, weekly and monthly. For some items, the number per month will vary and gradually increase from zero to a few per month. Here are some examples of topics for new agents:

- How will I learn? If I am investing one hour a day during my first few months to learn about my new industry and business, how will I learn? Will I watch videos from top real estate coaches and consulting companies? Will I take a top agent to coffee or lunch twice a week? Will I educate myself about inventory and spend one hour per day looking at new listings on the market?

- Where do I put leads so I remember to follow-up and call them in the future? This is a very critical basic system. The lack of this system allows agents to waste lots of leads. At first, your system may be a paper folder with one sheet per lead. Sooner or later, you will get a database. You should get a database system within one month of becoming a new agent.

- How do I process a listing?

- What do I need to do to close a deal after I get a signed contract?

These questions may seem very basic and even silly. At the beginning, there are many things you don't know how to do. Once you do them the first time, it may be days or weeks before you do it again. Are you going to re-invent the wheel or are you gathering notes on how to do things?

Salespersons and Systems

An interesting challenge in business are high energy agents who are amazing salespeople, who may know 1,000 people on Facebook and who may not be good at systems. In fact, they may be terrible at writing things down, or putting them in an organized place where they can find them later. We have worked with Hyper Harry salespeople who are amazing at meeting people, building rapport, and getting referral leads. They are just as amazing at wasting leads and letting them disappear into thin air.

Calm Cathy agents may have only 200 people on Facebook, but they are better with systems. They may organize those 200 people and send them a monthly email newsletter and mailed newsletter. Calm Cathys may be doing five times as much business as Hyper Harrys, but Calm Cathys may lack sales energy.

If you are a super salesperson but not a good systems person, do not worry. You need to buy services, use vendors, and buy systems to grow your business so you can focus on your unique talent. You need to hire people or vendors who are fantastic with systems. A good sign of a great assistant is someone who starts to create systems for your business without you even asking.

People

I will delegate other work to assistants, calling work to callers, and showing work to showing agents in order to become a Billion Dollar Agent who earns top profits.

The Billion Dollar Agent model provides a clear new industry model that will help you create a Billion Dollar Agent Business. You don't want just a team; you want a business, a Billion Dollar Agent Business. This model is very different than the typical assistant, buyer's agent, and listing agent team model you have read about and seen in other top teams. We introduce important new roles and concepts such as callers, showing agents, and leverage assistants. The buyer's agent model is dead. It does not work for 90 percent of teams. Most team leaders do not want to face the reality that their buyer business is broken and has very low profits. You want to fully leverage your business with assistants and callers; then you can add showing agents. At the Billion Dollar Agent level, you may have only one buyer's agent and a critical leverage assistant.

Staffing Takes Talent

You want to delegate everything you can. As discussed, you start with systems and add services. At some point, you are ready for staff. Do not get staff too soon unless you have the capital to do so or you are unable to do anything except meet and call. You need someone to organize your life from the very start.

Adding people is difficult and challenging for many businesspeople. In fact, it is the reason that many agents stay at $100,000 to $200,000 in GCI for 20 years instead of growing to $500,000. They are either afraid of adding people or they try, fail, and give up after a few attempts. Never give up.

When should I hire a part-time assistant?

We believe that all agents over $100,000 in GCI should have a part-time assistant using a budget of ten percent of their GCI. If you are at $100,000, you should spend about $10,000 per year, $20,000 per year at $200,000, and so on.

If you are between $50,000 to $100,000 in GCI and growing, you could benefit from an assistant. The issue is whether you want to grow faster and whether you can invest $5,000 for three to six months of help before it starts to pay off with more closed deals. If you previously ran a business or have capital, you should get an assistant before $100,000. You can do this when you start your business or when you get to $50,000 in GCI. Here are a few important points to remember:

- If you are over $100,000 in GCI and you do not have an Assistant, you are the Assistant and you make $20/hour.

- If you are spending less than ten percent of GCI on Assistants, you are under investing in leverage and slowing down the growth of your business profits.

Staffing Levels for a Billion Dollar Agent

There are three staffing members for a Billion Dollar Agent. We will walk through the three levels:

- **Solo -** Assistants and Callers - Grow from X to 80 deals per year

- **Team -** Showing Agents - Grow from 50 to 150 deals per year

- **Billion Dollar Agent -** Grow from 150 to 1,000 deals per year or a 20 percent market share in your area, whatever is greatest

Solo – Assistant and Callers

How and when do you grow from a one person operation where you help yourself to having a team of people that help you? Let's go back to the team color discussion of red, blue, green, and yellow.

You are likely red. You love being red. You hate when you have to do blue work. You slow down enough to be green so that you can be friendly, patient and answer questions, but you would rather be running at red speed. You are yellow enough to show buyers nice homes, but after spending ten to 20 hours as yellow, you will get tired of being yellow so much of your work week.

When you are starting out, even if red is your unique talent, you have to be all the colors of the rainbow until you start to delegate and leverage your time. It is time to delegate. You need blue.

Blue – Assistants and Systems

Your first hire should be a blue assistant. You also need blue systems, unless you are excellent at systems. If you are not good at systems and you hire a blue that does not have systems expertise, your business will be held back. You need both a blue assistant and blue systems from the start.

We advise agents to hire a part-time assistant for ten to 15 hours per week to get started. At $20/hour, that is about $995/month. Your first part-time assistant should start with following systems:

Step 1: Database Management, Lead Management, Marketing

- **Database Management** - Your database is the most valuable asset of your business. If you do not understand or believe this, you can close this book and go watch Netflix or surf the web. After working with many agents during the first few years, we made a decision to only work with agents who understand and believe that database management is a key to their business success. There are many solid database tools such as Top Producer, WiseAgent, Realty Juggler, Agent Office, eEdge, and others. We work with over 20 different databases. We can run a Billion Dollar Agent on almost any of them. Your database is organized by clients/SOI/vendors, seller/buyer leads, and agents.

You do not need to personally use the database to in order to run your business. We work with many top agents who have over $500,000 in GCI and they never go into the database. We run everything. Perhaps ten to 30 percent of agents are savvy enough on the computer to make calls directly from the database. For the majority, we provide printed Weekly Lead Reports which they can carry with them during the week. They can make calls from their office, their home or between meetings. All they have to do is mark up the sheets and we update their database.

- **Lead Management -** Every single lead is easily worth $100 in marketing value. Every single lead must be captured and entered into the database by your assistant. Lead capture is critical for the most valuable leads. Most Agents waste or lose leads. Top teams waste the largest number of leads. As you grow, the problem gets worse not better if you don't have a lead management system. If you get this correct when you are at $100,000 in GCI, you will grow faster and be more profitable than other agents.

  Every single lead must be coded properly by Seller – New Lead, Seller – A, Seller – B, Seller C or Buyer – New Lead, Buyer – A, Buyer – B, or Buyer – C. Each must be clearly assigned to a caller with a next call date and detailed notes from every call. Currently, less than one percent of top teams have their leads well organized. This is the Billion Dollar Agent system used by Best Agent Business and our clients. I have seen hundreds of top teams with databases that have only one type of buyer. They can have more than 500 leads under the buyer category with no clue of which ones are dead, closed, at a Buyer-A stage ready for showings, or pre-approved. There are also no reminders on when they should be called back. The industry is a huge failure at lead management.

- **Marketing -** Your assistant should start with a monthly email newsletter and mailed newsletter to all clients/SOI/vendors and seller/buyer leads in your database. This is the simplest and most profitable marketing which can be done. Until this is flowing, everything else can wait. We suggest you send an email newsletter around the first and a mailed newsletter on the 15th. For your monthly mailed newsletter, you can do a simple jumbo postcard, a generic mailed newsletter from various services, or something custom.

  Creativity may kill your business. If you fail to send anything out because you want it to be PERFECT, CUSTOM, or CREATIVE you won't send out anything. Another month will go by and your database will remain untouched. This is a big problem. This is a huge problem. We keep running into this problem.

  To make sure something happens, you need to start with generic newsletters or postcards. Keep it simple such as just listed properties, just sold properties, market statistics, a seasonal message, contest, or gift.

Please note that Step 1 involves activities that may not free up your time at the beginning. In fact, it may involve doing things you aren't doing at all, but these are the core fundamentals of your business. With solid database management, lead management, and marketing, your business will have a solid foundation to grow profitably.

Step 2: Listing Management, Closing Management, and Accounting

You are now ready for Step 2. Your solid database management system will help you streamline listing and closing management.

- **Listing Management -** Your assistant can take over 90 percent of the tasks needed to properly process a listing after you get a signed listing agreement. They may coordinate or hire other vendors to help with the signs, photos, and other services needed. Most importantly, they should implement our Billion Dollar Agent Listing Plan which incorporates every single free or low-cost listing marketing website or tool. The more powerful and complete your listing marketing is, the more powerful and complete your listing presentation will be. You will increase your ability to win listings.
  It is much better to have a listing plan which takes your assistant five hours to complete rather than one that takes you three hours. Those two extra labor hours may cost you $40 but they are likely to generate more buyer leads if you post it in more places on a regular basis. Your first few listings may have taken you ten to 20 hours each. Once you get to the Billion Dollar Agent level, a listing may only take one to two hours of your time.

- **Closing Management -** When you are new to the business, each closing is new and different. There is always something to learn. You are in charge of closings. Your assistant will help you leverage your time and reduce your stress by getting new closings set-up properly. You will have a checklist of action items for you and your assistant with due dates and a plan to keep you current. In short, you may be spending ten to 20 hours per closing from start to finish. With your assistant, your goal is to gradually move more of those hours to your assistant.

- **Accounting** - If you are over $100,000 in GCI and you want to become a Billion Dollar Agent with over $1,000,000 in GCI, you want to get basic accounting in place. It is far easier to get this going when your business is small. It should only take someone five hours per month to get your accounting current and produce monthly financials. This may reduce your overall costs during tax season.

Virtual Assistant or In-house Assistant or Systems Assistant

When you are ready to hire your first part-time assistant, you will need to make a choice between hiring a virtual assistant (VA), such as Best Agent Business, or an in-house assistant (IHA).

- **VA** - Virtual assistant who works remotely
- **IHA** - In-house assistant who works with you in your office

When speaking with someone about this choice, here are some questions I suggest you consider:

- Does your gut suggest that you would be a better fit with a VA or IHA? Why? Go with your gut.

- Is your physical office conducive to having an IHA? For example, if you work from a home office, an IHA is not a viable option. If your office does not have separate space for the IHA, will you hear each other on the phone? If so, it will make both of you far less productive. Does your brokerage charge you extra office rent to have an IHA?

- Do you like the idea of small talk and having someone to work with? Would you dislike having to talk with an IHA, hear about their life situations and what they did that weekend?

- Do you feel confident about your ability to recruit, hire, train, manage, and fire or would you prefer to delegate those tasks to a virtual assistant company such as Best Agent Business?

- Do you feel like you are good at systems and can create systems for your IHA to use or would you prefer to hire a VA company that already has systems they can implement for your business?

As the owner of a virtual assistant company, I have some personal bias on this topic. My gut is that for a first part-time assistant, about 70 percent of agents should hire a VA and 30 percent should hire an IHA. If you send me your answers to questions above, I would gladly tell you my gut about your situation.

If someone has previously had a few VAs or IHAs, they will already know what works and does not work for them. Someone may have had a few IHAs and realized VAs are better. Someone may have tried as few VAs, but it didn't work out and now they want to try the IHA approach.

Be very careful about hiring friends, family, or friends of friends. Are you going to be comfortable FIRING that person if they fail to perform? If you can't easily FIRE them, you should never hire them.

Be very careful about hiring other real estate agents as assistants. If they failed as agents, why do you think they would succeed at being assistants? In most cases, we advise getting a VA first and then when you are ready for the next step, you can hire a gopher.

Gopher – Courier

Driving around town wastes a huge amount of time for a real estate agent. The sooner you can delegate driving to a gopher/courier the better. Try to find vendors who do gopher work such as sign companies, photographers, and courier companies. It is always better to pay a vendor for a service that is their expertise than to hire an employee or contractor directly.

At some point, it will make sense to hire a local gopher for five to ten hours per week for $10 to $15/hour. They should be used for all business and personal gopher work. Make sure you tell them up front that they will be responsible for personal and business tasks.

Chunk your gopher work into one or two timeslots per week. We suggest that you set up a day and time to meet your gopher at your office to hand-off and delegate items. It is better to schedule this early so you do not disrupt your perfect day, focus hour and calling. Monday is a good day because you will have gathered personal items from the weekend and reviewed your gopher needs for the week. You can add another day if you need more than one day per week. Try to keep track of stuff that happens once a week or once a month.

If you are smart, you can easily free up five hours a week of your work life at a rate of $100/hour. That equates to $25,000 in additional GCI from this simple idea. Your assistant can and should help with recruiting, hiring, and managing the gopher. Let the Assistant manage the gopher, not you.

VA and IHA – The Best Combination

If you have a VA, and your business is still growing, we recommend that you add a gopher and then an IHA. Often, the gopher and IHA can be the same person, but not always. The exact, ideal combination depends on your specific situation. We recommend that an agent doing $300,000 in GCI try our Best Agent Business VA services for 20 to 25 hours per week and an IHA for ten to 15 hours per week. In other cases, we may recommend flipping that ratio.

Step 3: Callers – Green

As your business grows, you will quickly get to the point where you are not able to keep up with all the calling hours needed to call your seller leads, buyer leads as well as your clients/SOI/vendors. You will need more calling hours for your business. It does not matter if you are doing one, two or three hours of calling per day. If you need more calling hours, you need more calling hours. Stop wasting leads. Get more calling hours. You need green. You need callers.

When I started Best Agent Business, I did not plan on offer calling services right away. After the first few years, it became obvious that everyone was wasting leads. Buyer's agents were hardly calling leads and the industry needed more calling hours. We added a Calling Team who calls seller leads, buyer leads, expireds, FSBO, and clients/SOI/vendors. We have tracked over 500,000 dials over the last five years. We know calling.

Callers are a key vision of the Billion Dollar Agent model. Within the industry, some people call them ISAs or inside sales agents. Callers can be virtual, such as Best Agent Business, or an in-house caller (IHC). We will use the term IHC, just like IHA, to refer to an in-house caller.

Big Mistake – Getting a Buyer's Agent Too Early

The biggest mistake that agents make as they grow is hiring a buyer's agent too early. They may hire a buyer's agent before being fully leveraged with assistant help. They may hire a buyer's agent instead of hiring a caller.

If you hire a buyer's agent and they are not spending three hours per day doing outbound lead calls using a solid system, you hired the wrong person. They may be a showing agent, but they are not a viable buyer's agent. I will discuss this more later.

Callers Call Leads

Callers can be doing the following calling to leverage your time:

- **New Leads** – They can try to reach new leads two to five times in an attempt to reach them live. If you only are doing one to two dials, you are wasting leads.

- **Seller BC Leads** - Callers can call the growing backlog of seller leads who are unsure if they are going to sell or they can request a call back in the spring.

- **Buyer BC Leads** - Callers can call the majority of buyer web leads. This is FUTURE business and calling them monthly will nurture the leads.

- **Clients/SOI/Vendors BC** - Callers can touch base with your BC contacts on a quarterly basis if you are not able or willing to call. You should be calling the A rated people.

Business Size with Assistants and Callers – How Big?

If you focus on your unique talent and spend four hours a day meeting, two hours calling and two hours on other tasks, how many deals could you be doing per year? Let's assume you have enough assistant help to handle the volume of deals, listings, and closings. Let's assume you have enough lead flow and calling to produce the need for these meetings. Here are a few more assumptions:

- **Seller Deals** - Assume you have two listing appointments per week which last for two hours each. This amounts to 100 listing appointments per year. Those 100 listing appointments should result in 50 closed seller deals. You spent four of your 20 weekly meeting hours so you have 16 hours left for buyers.

- **Buyer Deals** - Assume you spend 15 hours per week meeting with and showing homes to buyers. If you have a 60 percent close rate, those 50 buyers should result in 30 buyer deals.

Does that sound crazy? Could you do 80 deals per year before you even need to have other agents working with you? Perhaps that is a bit high, it also assumes you have good seller lead flow. If you have a 70/30 buyer/seller split early in your career, it may be 50 to 60 deals total.

Showing Agents for Seller and Buyer Balance

As you grow your business, it naturally shifts from an initial buyer focus to more of a seller focus. Everyone in the industry agrees that top agents become listing agents and they focus on seller business for a variety of reasons.

Buyer Agent Model is Broken

When people hire a buyer's agent, they often end up paying someone $100/hour to perform three different roles which should be paid at a rate of $20/hour. Let's review a typical buyer's agent model.

If you asked teams with two to five buyer's agents for their total deal count last year, subtract out deals done by the business owner and divided by the number of full-time buyer's agents during the year, we predict you have an average of ten deals per buyer's agent. That is a joke.

If the buyer's agent is working full-time, that is 2,000 hours per year. If a buyer deal takes 20 hours and they spend 10 hours working with another buyer that did not close, we get an estimated 30 hours per buyer deal. Ten deals times 30 hours is 300 hours. A $200,000 sales price is worth $6,000 in commission. At a typical 50/50 buyer's agent split, that is $3,000 to the buyer's agent for 15 hours of work or

$150/hour. If your BA did about ten deals that took 300 hours of their year, what did they do with the other 1,700 hours of the work time?

I have had this discussion with a number of top team leaders and they usually end up laughing at the bar and then crying into their drink. Ask anyone who has a top team and has hired/fired more than ten buyer's agents to read this chapter and see what they say. The buyer's agent role should consist of three things:

- **Calling** - You need to make 200 dials to close a single buyer web lead.
- **Showing Agent** – They should be showing homes to buyers.
- **Closing Assistant** - This is the five to ten hours of closing work that needs done after buyers sign a contract. For some teams, a buyer's agent does this work. For others, the closing assistant does the work. It should always be the closing assistant.

Shift from Buyer to Seller Leads

As you grow, you will naturally focus more time and energy on seller leads and start to drop or ignore buyer leads if you don't have good callers or a lead management system. Here is how it happens:

- **Future Business** - If they are not a Buyer-A, you ignore them and you don't have anyone else that can work the buyer BC business. The buyer BC business is future business that will lead to more deals than the Buyer-A leads. That is the secret. Work the future business and stop wasting leads.
- **Unclear Motivation** - You work only very motivated buyers and ignore other ones such as potential job moves three to nine months out.

- **Unclear Credit** - You do not have a system to pass buyer leads to a solid mortgage partner for pre-approval.

- **Low Price Points** - You naturally focus on higher price points. After a while you ignore, do not pursue, or turn away other business below a certain price. For example, you may be in a market with a $200,000 average sales price and you start to turn away or refer out anyone at $100,000 or below.

Showing Agents hired at $20/hour will spend ten to 20 hours on a buyer side deal. If you qualify the buyer leads so 50 percent of them close, you will spend about $500 per deal on showing agent fees instead of the $3,000 BA split. You can do the buyer consultation in your office with the showing agent. Showing agents can also help with inspections, open houses, and some farm marketing activities.

Billion Dollar Agent Level

As you grow above the Billion Dollar Agent level of $1,000,000 in GCI, you will reach the point where you need to add the next two staffing roles.

- **Buyer's Agent** - At some point you may have more buyer consultations than you can cover. You may be 100 percent busy with listing appointments, or you may want to start delegating some of the buyer consultation work. If you have hired five to ten showing agents over a one to two year period, you may find one to two who have what it takes to learn the buyer consultation steps and provide guidance to showing agents. Each deal will probably take two hours. You can pay a flat $100 for those two hours of work. If you want to pay $200, that is okay, but anything more does not make any financial sense.

- **Leverage Assistant** - Billion Dollar Agent invented another new concept for the industry, the leverage assistant. The leverage assistant is a more experienced, systems-oriented assistant who helps you leverage your time and business. You may be paying $30,000 to $40,000 for a regular IHA. A leverage assistant is paid more, perhaps $50,000 to $60,000. They are your right-hand person for you and your business. They help you with life management. They make sure you focus on your unique talent and delegate everything else. The leverage moves the business to a whole new level where you can pursue the following ideas:

- **Group Meetings -** Marketing and team branding will lead to group meetings for expired seminars, FSBO seminars, client/SOI listing leads, and seller leads. You may meet in your office with three to ten seller leads without having to go on individual listing appointments.

- **Listing Assistant -** You will reach a point where you have a licensed listing assistant who may also be the leverage assistant. They will do all the pre and post-listing steps and coordinate your schedule. They will accompany you on listing appointments to complete paperwork, get MLS details, and go over the steps of your listing marketing. You can eliminate the prep work, spend less time at the listing appointment, and have everything done afterwards. In a perfect world, you may be spending one to two hours max on each seller deal.

- **Systems Assistant -** The leverage assistant or systems assistant constantly improves business systems or they help hire that resource.

Best Agent Business

Client Testimonials

Best Agent Business provides part-time virtual assistant and calling services to top agents. We help you focus on your unique talent and delegate everything else to grow your business.

"After 22 years in the military and 16 years in real estate I thought I was pretty organized, but Steve Kantor, the President and founder of Best Agent Business, and his team taught me that my real challenge was to STOP WASTING LEADS. Through common sense reorganization I've saved thousands of dollars a month. I'm no longer trying to buy more leads but working the good leads I already have. Their procedures have, as importantly, helped me create business that I would have otherwise lost; therefore, earning me thousands of dollars a month."

"I feel like I've hired Steve Kantor as a personal coach. He's gotten me to focus on the most important, neglected aspects of my business, which is not "wasting" the multitude of buyer leads that I didn't have time to follow up on. I knew there was "gold" in all those leads, but on my own I could not figure out how to mine that gold. Steve showed me how to do it, and so far I've got two appointments with buyers who I would have missed if it were not for his advice, systems and virtual assistants, who are doing their jobs with excellence and promptness. I normally can close about 50 of my appointments (sometimes it takes me up to a year to close them). Both of these buyers are in the $600,000 to $800,000 range, so I expect to bring in about $21,000 GCI from these three months of effort."

Stop Wasting Leads

Core Marketing

I will focus on core marketing to clients, SOI, and vendors with a monthly email newsletter, monthly mailing, and quarterly calling.

Your most profitable business is repeat and referral business from your core database of clients, SOI, and vendors. A Billion Dollar Agent spends the least amount on marketing to generate the most profitable deals. Most agents ignore and underinvest in their core database for a variety of reasons. A key aspect of achieving top profitability, using the Billion Dollar Agent Profit Model, is to focus on your core and maximize your marketing. We invented a new industry term called core because the concept goes far beyond past clients or referral marketing.

What is Your Core?

Let's start with some definitions of core to convey the concept:

- The central and foundational part of your business.

- A mass of iron serving to concentrate and intensify the magnetic field resulting from a current in a surrounding coil. Your core magnifies and intensifies your ability to attract and convert new leads to new clients.

- An arrangement of a course of studies that combines, under basic topics, material from subjects conventionally separated and that aims to provide a common background for all students. This is often called a core curriculum.

If you focus first on your core and your monthly email newsletter, monthly mailed newsletter, and monthly calling, you will establish a pattern that will positively impact your work on all seller and buyer leads. Your core is composed of three types of people:

- **Clients** - Clients are the people who have already done business with you. Clients include everyone who has already closed a deal with you. We never use the word past client because it has a negative meaning. Never use the word past client.

- **SOI** - SOI stands for sphere of influence. This can also be referred to as COI or center of influence. We keep SOI separate from clients because clients are worth more to your business. SOI is generally everyone you know, who is not a client, vendor, agent, or current seller/buyer lead who you feel comfortable marketing to. These are friends, family, and acquaintances. Most of these people are ones you have met at some point and they are also part of your mets database category.

- **Vendors** - Vendors are companies or individuals you work with, use, or recommend for your real estate transactions, home services, or other purposes. Some people call these service providers. We like to use the word vendors. Vendors are often not tracked well in a database and do not receive regular marketing information. Vendors are a valuable source of referrals and vendor marketing money for a Billion Dollar Agent.

Core Database

Your core database is the information on hundreds or thousands of people in your core. Since many agents are scared of the word database, we will refer to it as Core rather than core database to keep it simple. Your Core must be in a single database system such as Top Producer, Agent Office, WiseAgent, eEdge, or other database system.

Database Sources

You probably have far more people to add to your Core than you realize. At Best Agent Business, clients often start with 500 people. After a month of database management and cleanup, they have 800 people. Every single person is worth at least $100/year when you add them to your Core. Spend the time and money to add to your Core. Here are a few places we find people who were not in the main database:

- **Phone** - Your smartphone, iPhone, Android, or Blackberry likely has 50 to 200 people who should be in your database. These may be SOI, vendors, clients, and buyer/seller leads that got lost in your database shuffle.

- **Email** - Your email system, such as Outlook or Gmail, also has people who need to be added to your core.

- **Facebook** - You may have 500 friends on Facebook and there are lots who should be added to your core. You do not need to add other real estate agents. You do not want to add anyone who you are not comfortable sending a monthly email or mailed newsletter to.

- **Business Cards** - Do you have a stack of ten to 100 business cards of people you have met, who are not agents, who should be added to your core? They are each worth $100/year.

ABC Ratings

We code all people with an ABC rating such as Client – A, Client – B, Client – C. Here is a basic coding outline for your core:

- **A** – A person who has referred you people or if they are a client, they have done a repeat deal.

- **B** - You believe the person may refer you someone or consider you when they do their next real estate transaction.

- **C** - You are unsure if this person would refer you or consider you for business. It is very important to send monthly email and mailed newsletters to these people.

How much of your business is from referrals?

In real estate, most agents can give you an estimate of the percentage of their business that comes from referrals. People tend to use the words past clients or referrals. Across the industry, most people just toss out a number but they fail to dig deeper. Some people get 20 percent of their business from repeat/referrals, some get 50 percent, some get 90 percent. How do you know if you are getting too little or too much? We have analyzed over 1,000 agents and found the answers. Your business can be anywhere from zero to 100 percent from repeat and referral business. Most agents are in a range of 20 to 80 percent.

- **New Business / Lower Percentage -** If you are a brand new business, you will not have any repeat business. It may take you a while to develop referral business. Each year, your repeat/referral business should be growing. After your first five years of selling real estate, you should start to see a flow of repeat business.

- **Small Agent / Big Percentage** – The vast majority of agents who do three to ten deals per year have the majority of their deals from repeat or referrals. They do little or no marketing. Many agents below $100,000 in GCI may have 80 percent of their business from repeat/referral.

What is the proper percentage for a Billion Dollar Agent? Let's sort it out by using a Goldilocks approach. What is too low, too high, and just right?

- **Too Low / 20 Percent** - Agents who are getting only 20 percent of their business from their Core often have less profitable businesses. They may be overspending on marketing for new client leads, have a bad database or no solid database, and possibly have a love them or leave them attitude toward deals and clients.

- **Too High / 80 Percent** - Unless you are at the end of your career and business, 80 percent signals that your business is likely not growing. The owner may not be willing to implement enough calling of new Leads. The danger is that as the business owner ages and the database ages, the numbers will start to drop sooner or later through attrition.

- **Just Right / 40 to 60 Percent** - If you are newer and growing your business fast, you may be at 40 percent. For a solid Billion Dollar Agent, we suggest a target of 60 percent.

Billion Dollar Agent

Our target for a Billion Dollar Agent is to have 60 percent of their business from repeat/referrals based on the following:

- **Core, Client/SOI/Vendor, and Repeat/Referral** – Sixty percent of your business should come from these categories.

- **Seller Marketing** – Twenty percent of your business should come from proactive seller lead marketing such as farm, expired/FSBO, or other seller marketing.

- **Buyer Marketing** – Twenty percent of business should come from buyer leads generated from listing and buyer web lead marketing.

Fast Growing Business

A fast growing business will have a smaller percentage of business from their Core because the business is smaller and is investing in client acquisition marketing. In this case, the percentage may be 40 percent with 30 percent seller and 30 percent buyer.

Business Balance

Your business should be a balance of three types of revenue:

- **Core** - Fully work your core on all levels to maximize business profits and the long-term value of your business.

- **Sellers** - Sellers generate the best immediate profits for teams. The best ones are also buyers that give you a double deal. Some sellers are moving and leaving the area and thus will not be part of your Core.

- **Buyers** - Buyers are critical new clients for your Core, especially first-time home buyers who are more likely to refer others and who may move-up in five to ten years. Buyers may generate less initial profit if closed by a buyer's agent. Buyers treated well and moved into your Core provide important life-time value for your business.

Your Clients/SOI/Vendors are Leads – Stop Wasting Leads

Change your mindset and think of your core clients/SOI as leads. They are leads that are often wasted. Stop wasting leads. Your Core will convert at a combined rate of four to ten percent per year for repeat and referral business. For example, if you have 500 people in Core, you should get 20 to 50 deals per year.

Our target goal is ten percent conversion for Core with a marketing expense of only five percent. If you have 500 people, we want you to get 50 deals at $6,000 or $300,000 in GCI and spend about five percent, $15,000, or $30/person per year on marketing. Buyer web leads convert at a rate of one to two percent for most teams and five percent if you are doing amazing. Farm marketing converts at a rate of one percent or less. Since turnover may be five percent in a year, if you dominate the farm with 20 percent market share, you are getting 20 percent of five percent. This is one percent per year.

Why are you spending money and time calling buyer web leads and not calling your Core? Why are you mailing monthly farm postcards to your farm and not mailing monthly to your Core? Stop wasting leads. Until you are fully marketing to your Core, you should not spend time and money generating, calling or mailing to leads.

How Much is Your Core Worth?

Let's walk through how much one person in your Core is worth per year in GCI. We will start with our assumption of $6,000 in GCI per deal. If four to ten percent of your Core converts to closed deals per year, each person is worth $250 to $600 per year. That is an amazingly high number. Every single person you meet and add to your database as a SOI – B or SOI – C is worth $100 per year easily.

Do you see why it is so important to track down every single person you should add to your Core and do Core marketing to? Spend the money to track down all possible emails, phone numbers, and mailing addresses.

A key reason why we separate out clients, SOI, and vendors separately and then code them further with A, B, C ratings is so you can spend different amount of marketing money and time with each group. If you have 1,000 people and they are worth $500/year, you are likely getting $500,000 in GCI per year from your core. Some are worth more and some are worth less.

- **Client/SOI/Vendor** – A - Core people who refer your business may be worth $1,000/year in GCI. For example, if you have 100 people rated A and they refer you 15 deals, they are worth $1,000 each in GCI.

- **Clients** - Clients who have done business with you and are happy are highly likely to work with you in the future if you keep in touch with your Core marketing. We will estimate $300 to $500/year.

- **SOI – BC** - All of those people are doing real estate deals at a general turnover rate for your area, such as five percent. If you get 40 percent of their business, this would be about two percent per year or two percent of $6,000 equal to $120/year of GCI.

Types of Core Business

Core Marketing is seeking to generate the following types of business:

- **Referrals** – This business stems from introductions and connections to new leads. This number is usually larger than repeat business.

- **Repeat** – These are clients who are doing business with you again.

- **First Deal** - This is an important concept which people do not realize. First deal refers to a SOI ABC who has never done business with you before and does their first deal with you and becomes a client. Your Core of SOI is like a demographic farm of people you know or have met. It will, and should, convert at a higher percentage than farm marketing to people you do not know.

- **Vendor Marketing** - This is another new concept that involves joint marketing with vendors. Many top agents who do radio advertising have vendors that pay for some, or the majority of, their radio advertising. For your monthly mailed newsletter, we like to see one vendor pay for the mailing for one month. For custom newspapers, vendors can help pay for advertising.

- **Your Vendor** – This is a person who has either given you referrals or helped you do joint marketing.

- **Your Vendor – B** –This is a target list for joint marketing and referrals.

Farm Marketing – Seller

I will build farm marketing systems to dominate a 20 percent market share of increasingly larger farm market segments.

Farm marketing is effective seller marketing for agents who can get monthly farm marketing mailings flowing consistently. They should start with expired and FSBO marketing and only add farm marketing once they have achieve a 20 percent market share of expireds or FSBOs. If an agent is laid back, they should start farm marketing as soon as they can spend a few hundred dollars per month mailing to a few hundred homes.

Farm Marketing Choices

Farm marketing is usually marketing to a geographic farm of a certain neighborhood or area. There is also demographic farm marketing, such as apartment owners to find first-time buyers, higher-priced homes in a city, or short sales. Like most aspects of a Billion Dollar Agent Business, top agents have a huge advantage over other agents when they pursue farm marketing.

- You have the business size, depth, and capital to invest $1,000 to $2,000/month in long-term farm marketing for seller leads without needing any return on investment for one year.

- You have the focus and systems to make sure that a regular monthly mailing to your farm is flowing smoothly.

- You have systems to leverage listings in your farm such as neighborhood open houses and calling to create marketing awareness.

- You have the control to choose your farm and seek to raise your average sales price to increase your profitability.

Farm Marketing Analysis

To get started, we will identify some questions that will help you select a farm and farm activities.

- What is my current situation and revenue potential for a farm?
- What area should I be farming?
- What sales activities should I pursue?
- What marketing activities should I pursue?
- How much should I budget?
- What is my expected return on investment and revenue generated?

Levels of Farm Marketing

Depending on the level of the agent, farm marketing may involve one or more of the following levels:

- **Neighborhood of 200 to 500 Properties** - A neighborhood could be a condo building, or a development of homes.

- **Community of 500 to 1,000 Properties** - A community is often a few developments or a small area that is referenced and known as a specific area in MLS and web searches.

- **Area/City of 1,000 to 10,000 Properties** - An area or city is a larger group and often one of the most profitable for top agents in small cities or communities. In small areas/cities of 2,000 to 10,000 properties, there is often no competition from other top agents. Billion Dollar Agents can ultimately achieve a 20 percent market share of cities with a population of 10,000 to 50,000 people.

Turnover Rate

Almost all real estate agents are confused about how often people move. If you ask an agent how often people move, they say every five to seven years, which would imply a turnover rate of 14 to 20 percent. The problem is that number includes renters who do not own a home. For most farm areas, the annual turnover rate is two to ten percent with an average of about four percent. For 1,000 homes, there may be four percent or 40 homes sold per year. To choose a farm area, it is important to analyze multiple potential areas and see recent turnover rates. A farm of 1,000 homes with 80 deals per year is better for marketing than 1,000 homes with 20 deals per year.

Market Share by Agent

Do not assume that any agent has or does not have a significant market share in a farm. The only way to determine market share is to export data from the MLS and analyze it. We recommend exporting all the listings from the past three years to Excel. This will allow you to analyze not just closed deals, but listings which expired, as well as the shift in recent years. You need to export the listing date, closed date, listing price, sold price, listing agent and listing broker. Using a simple pivot table in Excel, you can quickly analyze counts and sales volume by listing agent and listing broker.

Usually, no agent has a 20 percent or larger market share of a farm area. In fact, often no one even has ten percent. If someone is over 20 percent, it may not make sense to pursue that farm area because it may take longer to establish a market share.

Budget

How much should you spend on farm marketing? We advise you to spend 20 percent of your marketing budget on farm marketing. If you are spending ten percent on marketing, that would be 20 percent of ten percent or two percent of your GCI. For an agent doing $500,000 in GCI, that would be about $10,000/year.

We advise you to have a budget of $15/year for farm marketing for each property. For example, for 1,000 properties, the budget would be $15,000/year for all marketing mailings, online media, and assistant services to run the entire campaign. In general, budget about $10/year for a monthly mailing such as a jumbo postcard, and an additional $5/year for advanced farm marketing such as neighborhood open houses, adopting buyers in your farm, and other activities.

Farm marketing is a long-term investment. You should not start farm marketing unless you can spend money on marketing and not receive any revenue or results for one year. Farm marketing does not truly pay off for about three years. As a rough estimate, when done fully, farm marketing can result in a five percent market share for year one, ten percent in year two, and 20 percent in year three and onwards.

Farm marketing may have a marketing cost of 20 percent of your GCI. Thus, to generate $100,000 of GCI from farm marketing, you should expect to spend up to $20,000 with a lag factor of six to 12 months. Once you get to year three and onwards, the marketing cost may drop towards ten percent. In addition, unlike many marketing costs, the investment is an asset which has residual impact and value.

If you have been doing farm marketing, calculate your current marketing cost. If it is ten percent or below, that is fantastic and we recommend increasing your farm area or starting a new farm area. Farm marketing can help you raise your average sales price and generate more buyer leads at a higher sales price.

Old School Marketing

The old school method of farm marketing involved choosing a neighborhood without analyzing turnover, market share, or the ability of an agent to fund the marketing for one year or more. The agent would then start to mail monthly postcards, and do regular monthly mailings without variation.

Best Agent Business Farm Marketing

Our business model for farm marketing involves basic monthly mailings, with an additional focus on marketing within your farm and online.

Marketing Niches within Your Farm

- **People You Know** - You should have everyone you know in your farm coded separately. These people can provide you with marketing information on which agents are mailing regularly to the farm as well as help spread the word about open houses or community activities that you sponsor.

- **Adopt Buyers** - We advise you to proactively work backwards for up to one year and adopt the majority of incoming buyers who bought properties in your farm. We advise you to hand-deliver a welcome gift basket worth $20 one month after the buyer moves into your farm. You will establish yourself as the agent in that area and by the end of the year of monthly marketing, they will think you were their agent. We call and code these as SOI – Adopted Buyer. All these adopted buyers will be receiving your monthly email and mailed newsletter just like all of your clients.

- **Expireds** - If you are doing farm marketing, you should be a strong listing agent and pursue expireds. You should go backwards for a few years to review all expireds in the farm which have not relisted and sold. Note them separately for more frequent contact and call to identify if they still have a need to sell their home in the future.

- **FSBO** - For a FSBO in your farm, there are many proactive marketing steps you can do to help them in their efforts. Your goal is to perhaps gain a buyer side after they sell their home, get referrals because they are so impressed with your approach, get buyer side commission to bring a buyer to the FSBO, or have them list and sell with you if they do not succeed as an FSBO. These marketing efforts can include online efforts and placing your call capture number on their sign once they agree to a buyer-side, co-broker commission.

- **Open House – Borrow Other Agents** - If you are not fully busy, you can ask to borrow listings of other agents who have listings in your farm. You can do expansive open house marketing and meet more of the neighbors.

- **Open House – Neighbor Open House** - For your open houses, we advise that you hold a neighborhood open house. For the first hour you can provide refreshments. Have 100 to 200 flyers passed out with specific neighbor invitations before the open house. Every person in your farm that you meet, establish rapport with, and do ongoing monthly email/mailing marketing to is worth about $50 to your business. Thus, it is actually very valuable and useful to meet five to ten neighbors who are only looking and curious at your open houses.

Custom Newspaper

If you are working a farm area of 5,000 or more, you are in the zone of being able to do a custom newspaper. A custom newspaper enables you to get vendors to help fund the newspaper with and get people from the farm area to write articles. This is a very powerful combination which is being used by some of the sharpest top agents. The cost is about 60 cents per newspaper, about the same as a jumbo postcard.

Online Farm Marketing

We advise you to allocate 25 percent of your budget to online farm marketing and 75 percent for regular farm marketing mailings. Online farm marketing is relatively new, very few agents are doing it and there are huge opportunities.

Most agents are spending online marketing dollars to seek and generate buyer leads. Very few are proactively targeting farm areas to establish relationships and long-term seller leads. Many agents are doing blogging and social media but almost none are doing it with any strategy or clarity of purpose.

- **Blogging** - Your blogging efforts can have keyword focus and market statistic updates for your farm areas. You can have multiple blogs for each farm area.

- **Facebook Community Page** - You can establish the primary Facebook community page for your farm area. In a few years, having ownership of Wildwood Shores on Facebook may be worth more than www.wildwoodshores.com top placement on Google.

- **Video** - By doing short videos of your listings and your farm areas, you can place them on the web with proper video SEO (search engine optimization) efforts. Video is still fairly new to real estate. Using video can help you leap ahead of agents who have been online for years in an area.

- **Community Website** - If it does not exist, you can create, own, and leverage a community service website that you establish for a farm area. This can have vendors, job openings, articles written by neighbors, and more. In some communities, within one year, your website could act like an online community newspaper. With the huge changes in journalism, you could even create a 'hyper-local' online community website with user-generated content.

Farm Marketing Questions

To start the process, answer the following questions about your farm:

- What is the farm area and how is it defined? What is the neighborhood name, subdivision, and other criteria?
- How many properties are in the farm?
- What type of property (condo, single family home) is there?
- How old is the average property?
- What was the average selling price last year?
- How many total closed transactions have there been in recent years?
- How many current listings are there?
- How many agent (you) closed transactions have there been in recent years?
- How many current listings do you have in the farm area?
- What percentage of properties are renters/absentee home owners?
- Does the farm area have any home owner associations, community groups, shared community areas, newsletters, websites, community events, or anything related to groups of people within the farm?

Agent Analysis for Farm

- How many total transactions did you have last year in your business?
- How many total transactions did you have in the farm area?
- What was the mix of buyers or sellers in the farm area?
- Based on the above information, what percent of your business was in the farm area last year?
- For every transaction in the farm area last year, gather the transactions or active listings this year, the name of person, address in the farm, and add a few sentences explaining the original source of the lead and how you won them as a client and their current relationship level.
- How many people in the farm do you know?
- How many people in farm have you actually met, been introduced to by name, and made them aware you are a real estate agent?

Sales Projection for a Farm Area

Here is a sample sales projection for a farm area:

Number of Properties:	1,000
Transactions Per Year:	50
Turnover Rate:	5%
Average Price:	$200,000

Average Listing Commission:	3%
Total Sales in Current Year:	$10,000,000
Gross Commission:	$300,000
Market Share Goal:	20% of all transactions
Commission to Agent:	$60,000
Marketing Cost Percentage:	20% (assume budget of ten percent to spend on marketing)
Marketing Budget:	$12,000
Marketing:	About $12/year per property

Farm Marketing Actions

The following list includes a growing list of farm marketing ideas:

Market Research

- Export data from the MLS
- Export data from property tax records
- Data provided by title company and analysis
- Consumer data from INFOUSA
- Competitor research on any agent with over ten percent of the market share
- FSBO data
- Expired data
- Change of address records
- Web search for street names

Segments of Farm

- Renters who are potential buyers
- Absentee home owners/investors
- Clients
- Friends
- People you have met
- Recent buyers for adopted buyer efforts
- Influencers or community leaders

Door Knocking

- Provide property statistics report
- Invite to a community gathering
- Invite to an upcoming neighborhood open house
- Introduce yourself

Meetings

- Brunch at your home
- Dinner party at your home
- Welcome adopted buyers
- Group garage sales

Mailings

- Property statistics
- Postcards
- Letters
- Handwritten notes
- Magazines
- Neighbor open houses for listings
- Just listed and just sold

Other

- Buy some useful tools and offer free loans for neighbors

Summary

An agent will naturally progress from working with buyers to working with more sellers as the business grows. If you cannot hunt expireds/FSBOs, then you should start farming as soon as you can invest $200/month to send mail to 200 homes in a small area. If you can hunt, remember to identify when to start farming activities to balance your business and maximize long-term growth and profits. Whatever you do, do not start farm marketing unless, or until, you are 100 percent current on more critical items such as client marketing and lead wasting.

Expired Marketing - Seller

I will dominate expired marketing in my area with a 20 percent market share of all expireds which relist and sell with a different agent within one year.

Expired marketing is a key profit pillar for a Billion Dollar Agent. All Billion Dollar Agents should fully commit to expired marketing sooner or later. Expired marketing is best done by a strong, well-established team with solid listing expertise and a successful record. Expireds are preferable because they are seller leads and therefore more profitable than buyer leads. Expireds can be done with a focus on raising your average sales price which also will improve profits. Expireds are listings which generates buyer leads for sign-calls. Expired success leads to more expired success with expired testimonials. Expired marketing done right is very difficult, so there is very little competition. The agents who only call expireds are missing the majority of expired leads because they are not able to reach most people on the phone. They focus on now business and fail to properly work future business.

Challenge to Billion Dollar Agents

Your goal is to get a 20 percent market share of expireds. You want to list and sell 20 percent of all expireds that list and sell within 1,000 days. If you do not have the patience and focus to work business that is 1,000 days out then you are a Hyper Harry doing a fraction of the GCI and profit compared to a Billion Dollar Agent. A Hyper Harry can only work now business and has no systems for future business. A Billion Dollar Agent will do about five times the net profit working fewer hours and less stress by working now and future business.

Expired Marketing Steps

- What business level should an agent work for expired leads?
- Stop wasting leads when you work expireds.
- Dominate expired marketing for $200,000 to $500,000 in GCI per year

Business Level for Working Expireds

It is amazing to see how many top agents used to work expireds in the past and now they do not. Over and over again, top agents would tell me that working expireds was critical to their original success in business. When I ask them if they still work expireds, they said "No." I assume they stopped working expireds because it was HARD and once they got successful they decided they did not HAVE TO work expireds anymore. Expireds are still out there generating millions of dollars of GCI per year in most large cities. It is an important profit pillar.

If an agent has a passive personality, they probably never worked expireds. Even worse, they may be over $1,000,000 in GCI and still not working expireds. It is simply another marketing system which should be added to the mix. Mailing to expireds is the same as farm marketing. You can always hire callers if you are not aggressive yourself.

If you are an agent who has an aggressive personality, you may have worked expireds in the past and perhaps stopped. It is time to restart working on expireds. You may have done calling and not done any mailing. You can hire passive people to send mailings.

Expired marketing is great because you have very little competition. Out of 1,000 agents, there is likely no more than ten that seriously work expireds. There is usually no one who works expireds properly using Billion Dollar Agent systems. It is very hard to do expired marketing properly.

Why is Expired Marketing so Hard?

Expired marketing is hard because it requires a mix of unique talents from three different people:

- **Database Management** - You need to organize and manage the constant stream of expireds, re-listings, and seller ABC leads generated from marketing efforts.

- **Mailing** - Expired mailings should be a combination of a long series of ten mailings over ten weeks, a larger 3D package-type mailing, and monthly jumbo postcards of expired, just sold testimonials to the entire database of expireds which are not relisted/sold yet.

- **Calling** - You want to try both hunter cold calling scripts as well as our innovative farmer market research survey scripts.

Most importantly, you need to be a super-strong listing agent and closer to close the sale and get the listing at the right price on a listing appointment.

Database Management

- Leverage tools such as REDX and Landvoice to properly pull the expireds for your market.

- Define your target market by area and lowest price. Do not exclude too many areas or low price points. Methods to profitably include working a broader area and lower price points.

- Never do this yourself. Have a top database person pull this information on a daily or weekly basis. The most critical aspect is monthly analysis of the market share and what percent of expireds are relisting and selling with the same agent versus different agents. Which agents are working expireds in your market at every level of competition?

Lead Management

- You must have a solid database and lead management system to track all seller leads as Seller - New Lead, Seller-A, Seller-B, and Seller-C. Overtime, some Seller-C Leads will become SOI-C if they choose not to sell. You need to differentiate between regular and short sale situations, between homeowners, absentee owners, and sellers that rent their property but still have a desire to sell within 1,000 days.

- For every expired who is now business, there is likely five expireds who are future business that will list within 1,000 days. Do you want to be one of the nine out of ten agents that ONLY work now business or the one in ten who works future business and becomes a Billion Dollar Agent?

- You must identify the different types of expireds for various ongoing marketing efforts such as short sale, renting pending a sale, absentee owner investor, and more.

Calling

- How much is it worth for you to have a ten minute conversation with an expired? It is likely you have never considered this question or figured out the answer. Once you do, you will be open to creative ideas that will get you the phone number of expireds or get them to call you.

- If you are doing one to two hours per day of calling, get an auto-dialer system such as Storm Dialer via REDX, Mojo, Vulcan, Phoneburner or other services. This can increase your productivity by two to five times but ONLY if you use it correctly. If you use it incorrectly, like most agents, you will fail to properly work future business.

- As soon as you speak with, or have email interaction with, an expired they become a live lead. You need to complete a lead sheet, give it to your assistant or send it to Best Agent Business to be properly entered in your main database. If you leave it in REDX or Mojo/autodialer, you are not managing your efforts properly. We can prove it.

- How much do you currently spend on your calling efforts for expireds? Many of you will say nothing because you are doing the calling.

- How much is your time worth? Is it worth $50/hour, $100/hour, or $200/hour? Let's say you think it is worth $100/hour and you call two hours per day. That is $1,000 per week times 50 weeks or $50,000 per year.

- I guess you are spending $25,000 to $50,000 on calling and nothing on mailing. Is that correct?

- I guess that out of 100 expireds, you are only talking live to 20 per month. The other 80 do not even know you exist.

Mailing

- Depending on your unique talents and current mix of your business, you should be calling, mailing or both.

- Most agents do not work expireds because they are not willing to call, they do not take rejection well, they are unorganized and could never put together a consistent mailing effort.

- Unless you have a minimum budget of $500/month for expired mailings and can invest without a return for six months, do not consider mailing.

- On the other hand, a Billion Dollar Agent doing $1,000,000 in GCI can easily be doing $250,000 from expireds with half of that from calling and half from mailing.

- If you are spending $50,000 calling 20 out of 100 expireds, wouldn't it make sense to invest a test of $10,000 to mail to 100 of the 100 expireds?

- We recommend a budget of $10 per expired to send them a series of ten mailings over a six months period.

Creative

- You can do a ten minute consumer research survey and offer expireds a $20 gift card for their time. This turns a cold call into a consumer research survey.

- You can organize expired seminars, where expireds will come to your office for a consumer focus group and receive a gift card of $50 or $100. The results will lead to listing appointments at a price which matches your starting budget criteria. The expired seminar will be a market research focus group and you will give attendees a $50 gift card to Wal-Mart, Barnes & Noble, Home Depot, or other major retailer. Your fellow agents will not believe that you had an expired come to your office or that you had multiple expireds come at the same time for a seminar. It is worth $100 to $500 for you to meet with an expired.

Expired Marketing Cost Analysis

Usually, agents only think in terms of how much they would pay for a referral fee, how much they would like to spend for marketing, and how much it costs to buy a lead. Let's review an expired at $200,000 for $6,000 in GCI.

- **Referral Fee** - Most agents would happily pay a 25 percent referral fee of $1,500 at closing. Please note that 25 percent is a very large number, but it is no risk because nothing is paid unless the deal closes. Smarter agents who are willing to invest cash in advance for marketing efforts seek to pay less than 25 percent.

- **Marketing Costs** - Overall, Billion Dollar Agents should spend about ten percent on marketing. For expired or farm marketing of sellers, they should spend up to 20 percent because it is more profitable and raises the average sales price which increases profits on the buyer side. This amounts to 20 percent of $6,000 or $1,200

- **Seller Lead** - How much would you pay for a seller lead? People are spending about $20 a lead to purchase buyer web leads. Some seller lead companies sell seller leads for $25 to $100. Often, they are about $50 to $75 each.

Let's invent something new, to figure out how much it is worth to speak to an expired on the phone or on a listing appointment.

- **Expired Listing Appointment** - Assume we spend $1,200 in total marketing costs. Assume you win 70 percent of your expired listing appointments and end up selling 70 percent of your expired listings. That means your close rate is 50 percent and an expired listing appointment is easily worth $600. To keep it simple, if you could buy expired listing appointments for $500 each, you would buy those ALL DAY LONG. It is worth giving an expired a $100 gift card to come to your office for a market research survey since more than one in five will end up becoming a listing appointment.

- **Expired Phone Consultation** - How much is it worth to speak to an expired for a scheduled 15 minute phone call when the expired is expecting to speak with you, answer questions about their situation, see if they qualify, or have you help them sell their home? We just proved that an expired listing appointment is worth $500. Let's assume that 20 percent or one in five expired phone consultations lead to an expired listing appointment in the future. You should be willing to spend $100 for an expired phone consultation ALL DAY LONG. Based on this, we invented our idea of an expired market research survey and gave them a $20 gift card for 15 minutes of their time answering questions about why their home did not sell.

Expired Marketing - Think Bigger - 20 Percent Market Share

What percent of market share are you getting of expireds that relist and sell with a different agent within one year? Until your number is 20 percent, the job is not done. Let's walk through the numbers.

- In your market, there are 500 expireds per month which fit your area and price criteria. For example, you only pursue expireds above $150,000.

- Of those 500, through research, we conclude that 100 per month are relisting and selling with a different agent within one year. That is your true competition. We do not care if they relist and do not sell, only if they sell. We do not care whether they relist and sell with the same agent.

- Of those 100 selling per month, you are getting three deals. It sounds good. Three deals per month, 36 per year, at an average sales price of $250,000 is about $200,000 to $300,000 in GCI. That sounds really good!

- That is good, but it is a tiny three percent market share. You could be doing $500,000 to $1,000,000 in GCI in expired marketing alone if you focus, focus, and focus.

- If you are spending $20,000 to $40,000 per year for less profitable buyer web generation, why aren't you spending that on expired marketing which is far more profitable and will generate more buyer sides with valuable sign calls?

- Why are you only doing three deals? Who is doing the other 97 deals? How much would you pay to get a ten minute phone call with an expired? How much would you pay for an expired listing appointment? No one in the industry thinks about these basic questions. The problem is the expired business is filled with aggressive salespeople and very few businesspeople.

Best Agent Business – Expired Marketing Services

Expired marketing is a huge opportunity for a select group of agents. We are gathering 1,000 agents over the coming years to dominate 50 percent of the expireds market share in the top 300 market areas. Best Agent Business will run the entire system including database, mailing, calling, and masterminds to share ideas. The target profit goal is 20 percent marketing costs for mailing/calling services. Thus, for every $20,000 spent on mailing/calling/assistant services, the goal is to generate $100,000 in GCI.

For every $10,000 invested in expired marketing, you can generate $50,000 in GCI. If you think you are killing it with expireds – you are wrong. Most agents doing $50,000 in expireds should be able to do $100,000 to $300,000 in expireds.

Buyer Lead Profits

I will build a big buyer business with solid profits for my buyer business.

You start real estate working with buyers. As your business grows, you get your first listings and start working with sellers. As you succeed, you focus more on sellers and less on buyers. You start to drop and ignore buyer leads that would have converted $5,000 to $10,000 commission checks a year or two ago. As your business grows, you may get buyer's agents and your buyer business will go from bad to worse. You may not even know your buyer business is bad because you just look at buyer deals, not buyer profits. At this point, you either abdicate business responsibility or you shift to the new Billion Dollar Agent system for big buyer business.

Buyer Business Vision

We believe that buyer business can be run as profitably as seller business for a Billion Dollar Agent.

Seller Business is Easy

Seller business is far easier than buyer business. As you grow your team, it is natural to move towards seller business and away from buyer business.

- **Fewer** - You have fewer leads with seller business. It is easier to manage and track. For many large teams, they may have 100 seller leads for every 1,000 buyer leads.

- **Faster** - Seller business moves faster. You go from inquiry to appointment much faster. It is more now business.

- **Funner** - Seller business is fun for a salesperson. If you priced the property correctly, you get the salesperson surge of closing a deal when you get a signed listing agreement. You are fairly confident the property will sell at that price. With buyers, you go through many time-consuming and emotional steps from inquiry to a closed deal.

Buyer Business Overview

We provide a top-level view of buyer business and then have separate chapters on the following:

- **Buyer Open House** - This highly profitable market segment is ignored by the majority of large teams. Unfortunately, they would rather purchase buyer web leads that convert at a rate of one to five percent instead of buyer open house leads that convert at a rate of ten to 20 percent.

- **Buyer Sign Calls** - A key profit value of your seller leads is buyer leads generated via buyer sign calls. As soon as the buyer sign call moves from the lead agent to other agents, the conversion rate drops and leads are lost. The majority of buyer sign calls are wasted including 800 IVR systems such as Arch, Proquest, AMS, Buyer Acquire, Voicepad and others.

- **Buyer Web Leads** - Many top teams purchase buyer web leads from Zillow, Trulia, Realtor.com or big buyer business systems such as Agentjet, BoomTown, Commissions Inc, Kunversion, Market Leader, Prodigy, Real Geeks, Real Estate Webmasters, Success Websites, and TigerLead.

We have a detailed version of a transformational showing agent model. This is one of our ideas.

Typical Lifecycle of Agent and Buyer Business

New real estate agents often work mainly with buyers, doing open houses, getting buyer referrals from their broker, or other agents in the office who do not want to work with buyers, and doing buyer relocation referrals.

By working with buyers, you will get exposed to inventory, buyer needs, and other aspects of the real estate business. Most importantly, you will build up your client database of people who may refer business to you, or need to sell their home in a few years. As a buyer in your early years you often drive the start of your seller business down the road.

The more buyers you work with, the more at-bats you will experience in terms of converting a buyer on the phone to a meeting, first meeting, buyer consultation, showing properties, writing contracts, and getting a deal to closing.

As you progress, you learn more about the business and how everyone who is super successful is a strong listing agent and has a solid seller business. You will work to develop your seller business, and get your first few listings.

As you grow to a pace and volume which keeps you very busy or too busy, such as 30 to 60 deals per year, your time becomes more limited. If you fail to get enough assistant help, you are stuck doing buyers, a few sellers, and lots of assistant work.

If you get enough assistant work, you find yourself jumping on the seller leads faster because a seller deal may take you only ten hours and a buyer deal takes you 20 hours. Seller leads also move faster to an appointment and buyer leads build in your pipeline for future business.

You start to let your buyer business go downhill:

- **Price** - If a Buyer is below $XXX, you are less interested and make the calls needed to win that buyer business. Each year, that $XXX amount may amount to $100,000, $150,000, $200,000 or more.

- **Future Business** - If a buyer is not ready right now, they are a Buyer – B or Buyer – C who may be three to 12 months out. You may let them drop on the floor, fall through the cracks, or throw the lead in trash which means that someone else is going to get a $6,000 commission check and it is not going to be you or your business. The failure to manage future buyer business is an initial step of going down the wrong road.

- **Tired of Running** - It is tiring to run around town and show homes to buyers. That is a key reason why many agents fade away from buyer business without hiring someone else to show properties.

- **Referral Agents** - You may think you are solving your problem by referring out some or all buyers to referral agents. This is usually not viable because the referral agents are not going to work hard enough to win the business. You do not have systems to hold them accountable, and track the leads. You just gave away the entire lifetime value of the buyer which is the MAJORITY of the net profit your business should be getting from that buyer lead.

What happens next? Agents usually decide to build a team and hire their first buyer's agent. Overall, I would fire 80 percent of buyer's agents. I believe that almost every top coach in the country would agree with a similar number.

- **First Buyer's Agent** - The first mistake is paying the buyer's agent a 50/50 split without thinking through why you are paying 50/50. If 90 percent of teams have a poor business model and overpay their buyer's agents, then you are just modeling failure.

- **Second Buyer's Agent** – If the first buyer's agent is not working out, you are getting busier, or you run into someone who wants to join your team, you may hire a second buyer's agent. It sucks more of your time and energy to keep an additional buyer's agent fed. You hand over a few more buyer leads that you would have worked yourself.

- **Marketing Expense for Big Buyer Business** - This is where it gets scary. Marketing is fun. Leads are exciting. You can buy leads. You can spend $1,000 to $3,000 per month and get 50 to 200 buyer leads per month. Many teams get a big buyer system which generates tons of PPC or SEO buyer web leads. You will feel like you need to feed your buyer's agents.

- **More Buyers' Agents** - Now that you are getting 100 to 300 Leads per month, you realize that leads are being wasted and you try to hire more buyers' agents to solve this problem.

Questions

There are no easy answers to the following questions:

- When do you stop calling a buyer lead? Are you making zero dial attempts? Do you make ten dial attempts?

- We can prove that if you make five dial attempts instead of two dial attempts you will reach twice as many live answers. If you work the leads, you will close twice as many deals.

- How many dial attempts do you or your agents make to a typical Zillow, Trulia, or Buyer web lead?

Riddle

How many calling hours are completed by a team of five buyer's agents who call for zero hours a day? How many dials does it take to close one buyer web lead? How many hours of calling does it take to make that many dials? What do you call a buyer's agent who does not make two hours of calls a day? The answer is an overpaid showing agent.

Profit Per Lead – PPL

What is your profit per lead? What is your PPL for buyer leads? For every buyer lead you get, how much profit do you make? If you run the numbers, you may be surprised by the result. This is a new concept for every single person reading this book. Your profit is determined partly by the average sales price in your area and by your ability to run your buyer business profitably.

The Profit Model of a Buyer's Agent is Broken

Our concern is that the buyer business of many teams is broken. Even if the team closes 25, 50 or 100 buyer deals via buyer's agents, the profit may be zero or very low. Let me walk you through an analysis. Here is a sample budget model for a large team with low profits:

- **Brokerage** – 10 Percent - Paying $100,000 on $1M in GCI because of overpaying brokers or paying for the splits/caps of the buyer's agents.

- **Marketing -** 20 Percent - Overspending on lead generation and wasting leads.

- **Assistants and General/Admin** - 20 Percent - Let's assume this is a normal figure.

- **Buyer's Agent Split**: 50 Percent

These figures may not be exact, but you can see a buyer business model with low or zero profits. It really does not matter if you get more leads, more buyers' agents, or close more buyer deals; you are still going to make almost no profit.

For more advanced teams, they may be adding a caller, often called an ISA (Inside Sales Agent) to help with buyer conversion. In many cases, the caller is added simply because the buyer's agent will not do the jobs they were hired to do, which includes spending two to three hours per day calling the buyer leads. In our view, the calling role should end up being about ten percent of your GCI.

When adding a caller/ISA, the proper way to handle the budget is to subtract the caller cost from the buyer's agent split. If a deal was via a caller, the buyer's agent may get 40 percent instead of 50 percent. This does not solve the problem of overpaying the buyer's agent, but it may lead to more deals closed.

Sometimes the caller cost is split between the business and the buyer's agent so the 50 percent has another five percent paid by the owner for a total of 55 percent. The worst possible situation is when a caller is added and the cost is not subtracted from the buyer's agent so you end up paying 60 percent total.

Caller compensation is often a mixture of a base salary plus a bonus. If the volume is not high enough, even though you budgeted ten percent for caller costs, you may be paying 15 to 20 percent but only charging ten percent to buyer's agents.

The owner may also be spending management time on the buyer side of the business as well as a handful of buyer's agents. Let's assume your time is worth $200/hour and you spend one hour per day on some aspect of the buyer business or buyer's agents. You would be spending $200/hour times 200 hours or $40,000 of your time on the buyer side.

Bozo Buyer Business

Are you running a bozo buyer business? It is very frustrating. There is no shiny squirrel you can buy to make it magically better. Business is hard. Buyer business is hard, but the profits are solid with the Billion Dollar Agent model.

Manifesto Statements

Here are some manifesto statements related to buyer business:

- Marketing is fun and easy, but the more you spend on marketing to generate buyer leads, the more likely it is that your profits will continue to shrink unless you have a buyer profit model.

- Shiny squirrels are fun. You can go buy the latest and greatest buyer lead generation tool, but this is not going to solve your problem. Your problem is deep and serious.

- More leads equals less profit per lead. The more buyer leads you generate, the lower your profit per lead will be wasting more and more leads. The best leads are going to be lost in the shuffle.

- Selling is hard. Calling is hard. Marketing is easy. Doing the sales work of calling is hard. It is hard to hire, hard to manage, and hard to run a calling system.

- Calling is harder than showing. It is far easier to find showing agents who can show properties than to find capable people to call leads. Your personal ability to qualify and convert a buyer on a first call is one of the most valuable skills you have.

- Buyer systems are as good as listing systems. You have incredibly solid systems for seller business with pre-listing steps, listing packages, listing appointments, and listing management. You need to have a solid buyer system which is just as structured to generate buyer profits.

- Buyer consults are as valuable as listing appointments. Spending one hour in your office for a buyer consultation with the buyer and your showing agent is as valuable as a listing appointment. The plus is you do not need to leave your office.

I Love Buyers – Buyer Business Lover

If you have been paying too little attention to your buyer business and are ready to commit, it is time for you to say "I Love Buyers." Act like you mean it and create buyer systems which are just as good as your seller systems.

Buyer Profit Model

The Billion Dollar Agent approach includes the following:

- **Systems -** The database management and lead management systems must be solid so that no lead is wasted and balance is maintained between marketing and sales calling. Marketing systems make sure that buyer leads are being touched with email and mailed newsletters. Buyer systems make sure that showing agents are doing their job properly and that buyers are moving smoothly from buyer consultation to closing.

- **Calling -** Calling is fully staffed with enough callers and hours to cover all new pipeline leads. The calling may be done by a combination of you, your buyer's agents, Best Agent Business callers, and in-house callers.

- **Showing Agent -** Showing agents are hired part-time at $20/hour or a rate appropriate for your market. They follow our showing agent model for a profitable buyer system.

Your Role for Buyer Business

It is time to make decisions. What are you going to do? Choose one or more of following:

- **Ignore Reality** - Throw out this book and delete any future emails about Billion Dollar Agent so you will not be reminded of the major business problems in your growing team.

- **Sellers Only** - Stop spending so much time and money on the buyer side and shift resources to sellers. Stop spending a few thousand a month on generating buyer web leads and move that marketing money to seller farm, Expired/FSBO, or radio marketing efforts.

- **Improve Buyer Side** - Agree with our manifesto and start making small steps to improve the buyer side of your business.

- **Delegate Buyer Business** - Hire Best Agent Business to run your buyer business operations or hire someone in-house who is compensated correctly. The person running a buyer business internally should be paid between $30,000 to $80,000 depending on your market and their results. This is not a sales position; this is an operations, systems, and management position.

Buyer Open Houses

I will leverage open house marketing to meet more people faster.

Open house marketing is often an extremely profitable marketing segment for buyer and seller business. If you are not doing open houses in a market where open houses usually get five to 20 people, you are missing out on a huge opportunity. If you do open houses and they are productive, you can easily double your business from open houses using our Billion Dollar Agent model. Each market is different based on local practices, time of year, and market conditions. If you dislike open houses and never hold open houses, you may want to consider running one open house per month as a marketing test. If you like open houses, you can do fewer open houses and produce more business by spending more time and energy on the pre and post-open house stages.

Why Should You Do Open House Marketing?

Sellers think an open house is held to help sell their home. A real estate agent thinks an open house is held to perhaps sell the home and find potential new buyer leads. A Billion Dollar Agent has a much broader perspective:

- **Seller Marketing -** By hosting a huge open house, a Billion Dollar Agent is showing the seller their commitment to marketing their home to prospective buyers. By putting out 15 to 20 signs instead of three to eight signs, more people will be aware of the marketing effort. Before the open house, 100 to 300 flyers are distributed to neighbors to invite them to the open house and 100 neighbors are called by an agent to invite them and see if they know anyone who may be looking to buy a home. One-hundred to 300 neighbors, potential buyers, and potential future sellers will all aware that you are an agent who does the best open house marketing of anyone in the area. This will help you get future seller business and win at competitive listing appointments.

- **Seller Leads -** Our goal is to identify or nurture seller leads from an open house. Some of the buyer leads will also be seller leads. The impressive open house will make sellers consider you to sell their home. If you do a neighborhood open house before the public open house, you will get neighborhood real estate sneezers. A sneezer is the person in the neighborhood who knows about all the homes for sale, people moving, primary real estate agents in the farm, and more. They constantly spread neighborhood gossip about homes for sale, agents, and prices. You will also get neighbors who most Agents would consider to be 'just neighbors looking' and ignore. The neighbors looking at an open house may be 20 percent more likely to list and sell their home within a year compared to five percent of the overall population. You should treat them as a SOI – C leads until you speak to them further.

- **Buyer Leads -** The best possible lead is a buyer lead looking to work with an agent. The next level lead is a buyer lead that is future business and has a 20 percent chance of buying something within a year. The third level is a now buyer who says they are currently working with an agent.

Letter to a Friendly Hyper Harry Open House Loving Agent

The interesting thing about business is that often the balance you need is missing. Someone may ignore open houses when they should be doing open houses. Someone who is doing open houses may need to balance their efforts to get more long-term results. Hyper Harry agents are very friendly and outgoing. They often do great with open houses, meeting people and developing rapport, but they could do so much more if they had Billion Dollar Agent systems to fully work leads. Here is a letter to one of those Agents.

Dear Joe,

Focus. Focus. Focus. Slow down and focus. Print this letter out and read it over a few times a day when you are calm and quiet. Focus on your unique talent.

I do not know you very well yet, but I am going to take a chance and muse a little about you and your unique talent. You are a Hyper Harry. People love you. You have tons of energy. You love to talk. You love to meet with people. You love to build rapport and help people. People love to give you referrals.

Our goal is simple. We want to have you meet with people for as many hours per week as possible, without getting burned out. Then, we want you to call for two hours per day. One hour per day should be spent calling your seller/buyer leads and the other hour is for calling to chat, say hello, and schedule meetings. The only purpose of this one hour of calling per day is to schedule meetings with people such as clients, SOI, and vendors for coffee, lunch, drinks, or dinner.

Your working life should be composed of only three things: meeting, calling, and other. Calling means outbound calls to people or Leads. You are probably spending your time as follows:

- Meeting – 15 hours
- Calling – 3 hours
- Other – 30 hours

Our goal going forward is:

- Meeting – 30 hours
- Calling – 10 hours
- Other – 10 hours

Block out days of the week and times of the day for meetings with clients, SOI, vendors, and first-time buyers. Start sending emails and making calls. Book your schedule two to three weeks in advance. The best meetings, in priority order, are for a listing appointment, buyer consultation, open house, buyer showings, client/SOI, and vendor.

Open House Overview

Real estate, like most small businesses, makes it easy to become overwhelmed with the wide variety of marketing tactics and operational details needed to run the business and close a deal. The sooner you narrow marketing tactics to just a few and delegate everything else, the better it will be.

Billion Dollar Agent Bushido

- Focus on what is working and go deeper
- Restart what worked well in your past
- Delegate what you hate

Focus on What is Working and Go Deeper

Most of the time there are one or two parts of your business that are going quite well. Unfortunately, most agents do not go deeper and they have no clue how deep they can go. For example, if you ask any agent how many client/SOI repeat and referral deals they SHOULD be getting from 500 clients/SOI, they will likely have no clue. If they are getting 20 deals per year for 70 percent of their business, they may tell you that 70 percent of their business comes from client marketing. The problem is that they should/could be getting 50 deals or ten percent instead of 20 deals and four percent.

If you do great open houses for one week a month and then start doing open houses for two weeks a month and you create a true system, you could get four times as many deals from open house efforts in the coming year.

If you are getting $100,000 in GCI from expireds and it is working well, and your Billion Dollar Agent target is $500,000, then keep going, go deeper, focus on expanding that revenue pillar.

Restart What Worked Well in Your Past

In interviews, I often hear BDAs mention that they used to do open houses, FSBOs, or send a monthly mailing to their client/SOI. For a variety of reasons, they have stopped what was working well in the past. If something was working in the past, go back and get it started again. You do not have to be the person who does all the work; just get it going and delegate.

Delegate What You Hate

Let's say that you hate open houses. Given your market, listing inventory, and staffing for agents, running open houses could be a very good thing to do. In fact, it is very likely that you are overspending on buyer web leads and under spending on open houses. Perhaps you hate open houses and feel they are a waste of time.

You hate FSBOs because they are unrealistic, because they are angry at the previous real estate agent. I bet you love getting a listing appointment with a motivated seller. Delegate what you hate, such as working with FSBOs and expireds and let a system ran by other people work those marketing segments. Focus on producing listing appointments with motivated sellers.

For every BDA at $1,000,000 in GCI, we can usually identify $500,000 to $1,000,000 of missing GCI due to a total lack of basic revenue pillars such as FSBO, expired, farm marketing, open houses and other marketing tactics.

You likely got tired of doing listing management early in your career, so you delegated those two to five hours of posting photos and virtual tours on a billion websites and hired an assistant. Then you began to hate closing management so you delegated that task. After a few years, you began to tire of showing homes so you delegated to a buyer's agent. If you like meeting with people, but do not like setting up and taking down ten to 20 directional signs for every open house in bad weather, just delegate it. Delegate what you hate.

Time or Money?

Do you have more time or more money at this stage of your business? Most of you start the business with very little money or capital to invest. You have time. Most new real estate agents waste their time and do nothing at all. Salespeople who need to make a living or want to make a killing, hit the phones or hit the streets.

If you are a newer agent, you may have more time than money. If you are a top agent, you probably have more money than time. This is good and bad. It is good because you can delegate what you hate and hire systems, staff, and vendors to make things happen and grow your business. It is bad because it leads to buying the latest shiny new thing and overspending on marketing while you ignore the sales side of the business.

Meet or Call?

Do you prefer to meet with people or do you like to call people? Would you rather spend two hours calling five to ten clients/SOI or two hours meeting with one person? There is no right or wrong. What is the best ratio for you of meeting versus calling?

Would you rather have ten hours of meeting with people for one hour of calling, or would you prefer five hours of meeting instead of one hour of calling? These questions may seem unusual because you have never created a perfect day and developed the solid time management skills of a Billion Dollar Agent. A Billion Dollar Agent has a perfect day they follow. They know the current ideal ratio of meet, call, or other time which fits their unique talent and moods. They review weekly and Kaizen their perfect day.

Calm or Hyper?

Are you a Calm Cathy or a Hyper Harry? A Calm Cathy has no problem sitting still for an hour or two and moves and speaks calmly. A Hyper Harry cannot sit still, finds themselves driving around more than is needed, speaks fast, and always likes to be on the move. It is hard for a Hyper Harry to sit still and focus for an hour or two.

If you are a Hyper Harry, you should have a high number of meet hours. You may want to spend as much as 20 hours a week meeting with people. Meeting with people pumps you up, it gives you emotional energy, and you love it. In fact, you do it for free all the time whether you are selling real estate or not.

Time, Meet Hyper

At this stage of your business, you have more time than money. You like to meet people, and you have a Hyper Harry personality which dynamically allows you to build rapport fast with strangers you meet at an open house or anywhere in the world. About 50 percent of your business comes from open houses, and you are wasting 25 to 50 percent of current open house leads. You need to focus on what is working and go deeper, way deeper.

What is the Purpose of an Open House?

What is the purpose of an open house? Many consumers and sellers believe that the purpose of an open house is to get the home sold. As we know, miracles do happen, but not that often. Out of 100 open houses, how many led to a buyer who bought that house? When a miracle does happen, you should blow it out of the water in terms of publicity to hammer home the power of the open house.

- Have your seller mention their great agent who is super at open house marketing and actually found the buyer at an open house.
- Send a just sold postcard and mention the buyer came to your open house.
- Send a postcard to your target list of agents to borrow their listings for open houses and announce that you sold another home directly from an open house.

For a Billion Dollar Agent, the purpose of open house marketing includes:

- Finding buyers and sellers looking to buy within 1,000 days
- Building a database of SOI from neighbors or just looking people
- Raising the average sales price of an open house by focusing on higher price points

Open House Analysis – Billion Dollar Agent Profit Model

Does it make sense for you to do an open house?

- If you are doing $100,000 per year, or $250,000 to $500,000 in GCI, should you be doing an open house?
- How many should you do each year?
- What parts should you do versus delegate?

Let's dive deep and analyze how wildly profitable an open house can be for your business. Let's assume there is a $200,000 average sales price and commission check of $6,000:

- Organize and run your open house so contact information such as name, address, phone, and email are required. Offer an open house contest to help encourage the gathering of this information. If you fail to get full contact information, you defeated the entire purpose of the open house.

- Out of 100 people, 50 percent are neighbors or people that are just looking. Those 50 people are just as valuable as buyers. We call these people SOI-C unless you really hit it off with them and can then mark them as SOI-B. The neighbors who come to an open house are the ones who talk about real estate prices and agents with other people. They are influencers. They are sneezers. You want to impress them and have them tell other neighbors that you ran the best open house they have ever attended. Some of these people are THINKING of buying or selling in the coming months, year or two year period. We do not care whether they list their home in 100 days or 1,000 days. As long as they are in your database, getting your information and requiring quarterly calls to touch base, we know you will get a solid shot at their business when it comes.

- The 50 neighbors should lead to four to ten percent or two to five deals per year. That is $12,000 to $30,000 in GCI.

- Of the 50 buyers, about 20 percent are locked-up with other agents. Of the remaining 40 people, 20 will end up buying a home within 1,000 days. Your target goal is a 50 percent market share or ten closed deals of those 20 people. Ten closed deals is $60,000 in GCI. The prediction is a ten percent conversion rate from an open house lead. From ten open house visitors, you can expect to close one sale within 1,000 days.

- If you add all this up it leads to an estimated $72,000 to $90,000 in GCI from 100 open house people. To be conservative, let's knock that down to $50,000 for 100 people.

> That means every single open house visitor is worth $500 in GCI to you and your business.
>
> Read the last sentence a few times. If I had asked you, before reading the analysis, how much commission an open house lead generates, what would you have guessed? If the conversion rate of an open house lead is ten percent and your current conversion rate on buyer web leads is one percent, then why are you overspending on Buyer Web Leads?

In your situation, you estimated that you got about seven people at each open house in 2012 and hosted about 50 open houses. You had excellent success at gathering contact information for every person which is currently in a Google doc. So, you have about 350 people. Based on this, we would expect you to get 35 deals. You stated that you already got 20 closed deals for $120,000 in GCI. That is awesome! That is fantastic!

You spent about 250 hours doing 50 open houses and you already generated $120,000 in GCI. That is about $500/hour. The best news is that you wasted 50 percent of the leads. Yes, that is good news. It means you have a huge upside.

Open House System of a Billion Dollar Agent

Let's brainstorm a simple version of how open houses should work going forward. This is about ten minutes of brainstorming from someone who has never been a real estate agent and never hosted an open house:

Open House Budget

- **Joe Time** - How many open houses do you want to host per month without getting burned out? It is super critical that you be conservative. I would much rather have one open house with 20 people than two open houses with ten people each. Let's say you decide to do one per week or 50 per year.

- **Open House Days and Times** - Decide on which days of the week and which times of the day are best for an open house. Mix it up a little. Try different times on Saturday, Sunday, or during the week.

- **Marketing Budget** - We need to pay someone to handle the signs and to market, with flyers or postcards, to 100 to 300 neighbors before the open house.

Choose Listings for the Open House

- For each of your new listings, decide whether to hold open houses and how often.

- For your brokerage, review weekly new listings and focus on higher price points and the best locations to maximize traffic and signage.

- For FSBOs, start a marketing program to identify the best higher-priced FSBOs which are offering a buyer-side commission. Develop rapport and get buyer leads, offer to host an open house and invest $200 to $300 of your own marketing money.

Open House Flow

- Schedule

    - Create and maintain an ongoing database of all open houses completed, planned, or possible target listings.

    - Decide two to three weeks in advance, the open houses you want to target. Have multiple options so if someone goes under contract, you have a backup open house for that time slot.

- Prepare For and Hold the Open House

    - Have a showing agent at every open house or on-call for any hot buyers who want to see properties immediately.

    - Mail flyers or postcards to 100 to 300 neighbors so they arrive before the open house.

    - Send 100 postcards to sellers' friends/SOI if they are willing and interested in providing their lists.

    - Have sellers post the open house on their Facebook page.

    - Knock on the door of the closest 50 homes for one hour before the open house while your sign company puts up the signs.

    - Have a sign company set-up and take down ten to 30 directional signs using proven systems that maximize traffic for an open house.

    - Have a one-page, required registration form on multiple clipboards which mentions an open house contest for a $20 gift card. Have room at the bottom of the clipboard for you to make quick notes after they walk out the door to remember their situation.

    - Quickly rate people as Buyer ABC or SOI BC rating.

    - Do a quick video thank you before leaving. Post it on YouTube under your open house videos so you can easily email a link to every person on Monday morning. This will help them remember you, your face, your voice, the address, area, and home.

- Send all lead sheets to Best Agent Business by midnight of the open house so we can process, add to your database, and launch action plans.

- Follow-up Week One
  - Write hand-written notes to every person the next morning. You need to have 30 minutes blocked out. This is very important.
  - Mail out introduction packages for you and your business to Buyer AB leads two days after the hand-written notes.
  - Email everyone with a proper message and send a link to the thank you video.
  - Call the Buyer A leads ASAP. Call the Buyer B leads within a few days.
  - Make one dial attempt for every Buyer C and SOI BC leads.
  - We will make your other dial attempts if they are not reached.
- Ongoing Follow-up
  - Call Buyer ABC leads monthly or more frequently.
  - Call SOI BC quarterly.

- Delegate calling to Best Agent Business if you exceed your current calling hours.
- Send a monthly email newsletter.
- Send a monthly mailed newsletter.
- Invite everyone to monthly client marketing events based on their interests. Introduce them to other people they may enjoy meeting. Be the connector.
- Create a monthly seminar lunch or informal dinner for a maximum of three to five people to speak about the marketplace and their needs. Leverage your time using a group meeting.

Let's get started. We have 350 people sitting in Google docs who are not receiving the proper follow-up. Every week, you are losing $1,000 in GCI to other agents. Does that get your competitive juices flowing?

Best Agent Business

Client Testimonials

Best Agent Business provides part-time virtual assistant and calling services to top agents. We help you focus on your unique talent and delegate everything else to grow your business.

"How much per hour are you worth? Why would you be doing work that someone else could do for $25 an hour? Would you like to spend an extra hour with your family every day, or an extra day with your family every week? Best Agent Business is also about improving the quality of your life. It's about producing more, and profiting more in your business."

"Best Agent Business has made a tremendous difference in my business in the last 6 months. The biggest impact has been on my database. Steve Kantor and his team have helped me organize and systematize my database to make my Callers more effective. They have helped with calling back leads that I otherwise would not be able to get to, which lead to more listing appointments for my team and an increase to our bottom line. For anyone looking for rapid growth I would highly recommend Best Agent Business."

Billion Dollar Agent Vision

Billion Dollar Agent Profit Model

I will achieve the Billion Dollar Agent Profit Model target of 50 percent net profit on $1,000,000 in GCI for $500,000 net profit.

How much do you make in your business? How much should you be making? Do you know how much you are making? For simplicity, we will define your net profit as your salary equivalent. This is the amount of money you earn after expenses and before taxes. It is similar to what you would earn in a job.

After reviewing over 100 financial statements of Billion Dollar Agents, we have created the Billion Dollar Agent Profit Model. There are three levels of business and profits. A brokerage is usually a very poor business model with net profits of zero to 20 percent. Many top teams think they are a team operating a small brokerage business model. A team has a net profit of 15 to 40 percent. A Billion Dollar Agent business has a net profit of 40 to 60 percent.

Great News – The Secret to Increasing Your Business Profits

Billion Dollar Agent Manifesto includes a section on the Billion Dollar Agent Profit Model because almost every single top team we have spoken to wants to increase their net profit. We are going to answer the following questions:

- What net profit goal should I have based on my business size?
- How can I easily delegate monthly accounting and financials?
- How do I implement and achieve the Billion Dollar Agent Profit Model for my growing team?

Broker or Team or Billion Dollar Agent Business

Would you rather own a brokerage, a real estate team or a Billion Dollar Agent Business? If you are a Broker, do not get mad at me. If you are a top team, aspire to be a Billion Dollar Agent Business. If you are a combination of a broker and a team, then realize that you are running two businesses. Let's walk through some of these options.

Owning a real estate brokerage is often terrible. If you asked 100 new franchise owners whether they would do it again, the vast majority would say NO, it was a bad business decision. The ones who claim it was a good decision would be lying. Let us review their financials before and after they purchased the franchise.

A brokerage is run by a broker who is usually going broke. They just do not know it. Often, they are muddying their financial waters by combining their brokerage business with their individual team. Their team production is being used to fund the losses of the brokerage. For example, we have seen many brokerages which have the team making $250,000 and the brokerage losing $100,000. The owner THINKS they are making $150,000 because they do not want to face reality.

If you are running an independent brokerage, your reality depends on whether it is a brokerage of independent agents, a team within a brokerage, or some combination.

Profit Margins

The key is to focus on net profit margins, before owner compensation or draw so you can compare apples and apples. The net profit number is close to a salary equivalent. Assume we are examining a business with $1,000,000 in GCI. Here are some basic numbers:

- **Broker Average** - 5 Percent - The average broker makes a net profit below five percent. In recent years, the average is even lower than five percent. That would be a $50,000 profit on $1,000,000 in GCI.

- **Broker Good -** 10 Percent - A good brokerage that is running profitably may make a ten percent net profit or $100,000.

- **Broker-Team Combination -** 20 Percent - A business that combines a brokerage with a team may end up with a 20 percent profit margin or $200,000.

- **Team Low Profits -** A team with poor profit management will have a 20 percent net profit. There are Billion Dollar Agents out there with $1,000,000 in GCI and only $200,000 in net profit.

- **Team Average -** 30 Percent - The average top team is making a net profit of about 30 percent or $300,000 on $1,000,000.

- **Billion Dollar Agent Business -** 50 Percent - Our target goal is 50 percent net profit for a Billion Dollar Agent Business. That means $500,000 net profit on $1,000,000 in GCI. This number is adjusted lower or higher based on the average sales price in your market area. This target number assumes full implementation of our Billion Dollar Agent systems either by you, Best Agent Business, or a combination.

Let's analyze an independent brokerage which evolved from a top team to a good brokerage. The brokerage has 50 agents and they did $3,000,000 in GCI. That is $60,000 per agent which is pretty good. The net profit was only $260,000. That is a nine percent net profit. The net profit was better than an average broker, but far below a typical team. For example, a team doing $1,000,000, with an average net profit of 30 percent would have generated more net profit at $300,000. At the same time, there is a solo agent working with a showing agent business model who did $525,000 in GCI with a net profit of $300,000. That is more than the brokerage with 50 Agents. How can that happen?

How can a solo agent who doesn't sell properties or have any buyer's agents have revenue of only 20 percent of the brokerage but have a higher net profit? It all comes down to the difference between a brokerage, a team, and a Billion Dollar Agent Business. Which business do you think is worth more? Here are some tips for you:

- If you are a broker, face reality.

- If you are a broker or team combination, split your books. Run each business on separate financials so you can see how much you are making per hour on your brokerage and on your team. Decide what you want to do going forward.

- If you are a team, focus on net profit. Have monthly financials and forget about total GCI. Your goal is to increase your net profit 20 percent or more per year for the next ten years. If you do not know whether your net profit is bad, average, or good, find out by doing a Billion Dollar Agent Profit Model analysis.

- If you want to create a Billion Dollar Agent Business, you have come to the right spot. Read this book carefully, underline sections which relate to you, write me a long email or letter, and then let's talk.

In the beginning, there was a real estate brokerage. RE/MAX changed the model and focused on the top agents. Now Billion Dollar Agent is focusing on the one in 1,000 agents who do over $1,000,000 in GCI per year.

A Billion Dollar Agent Business can exist within franchises such as RE/MAX, Keller Williams, Prudential, Coldwell Banker, or they can exist as their own broker as a team-only model. At first, you aspire to create a team. After a few years and staffing changes of hires, fires, and quits of assistants, buyer's agents and inside sales agents, you will see my point of growing a Billion Dollar Agent Business instead.

The step beyond a Real Estate team is a Billion Dollar Agent Business. There are very few of these in the USA/Canada currently. For every one Billion Dollar Agent Business, there are about 100 real estate teams.

Profit Problems for Top Teams

There are common problems that we see across all teams. Here are a few of those problems:

Big Ego Brad

Big Ego Brad is always crushing it and killing it. It is someone who grows deals/GCI but not profits. Do you happen to know top agents who run a growing teams of $500,000 plus in GCI? They focus on growing 50 to 100 percent per year, but the focus is solely on growing deals, sales volume, or GCI. They focus on revenue growth and they ignore net profit.

After a few years, without the clarity of basic profit models, they may have doubled their GCI, but they worked the same hours with more stress and bigger monthly expenses. Their net profit is sometimes the same as when they were half the size. Did you catch that?

We have seen many top teams that went from $500,000 in GCI to $1,000,000 in GCI. The problem is their business is actually worth less money but they do not know it. A lower percentage of business is coming from client marketing of repeat/referral business.

Brad is sometimes a Hyper Harry and loves to go to conferences and brag about the growing size of his business. In private, Brad will usually tell me the details of his true net profit situation. In real estate, people talk about how many deals they did, their sales volume, or GCI.

People rarely talk about net profit. My company, Best Agent Business, works closely with growing agents and top teams to increase their net profit with the Billion Dollar Agent Profit Model.

Brad is always looking for more deals. He will spend thousands of dollars per month on buyer web leads, and hiring more buyer's agents. He may not realize that based on his business model, he is actually making no profit on a buyer web lead deal. There are hundreds of teams in the country that are closing ten to 50 Buyer web lead deals per year. They do not realize they are making zero profit when you add up brokerage fees, marketing costs, ISA-caller costs, buyer's agent splits, assistants, and general administrative costs.

Big Ego Brad loves to have the latest and greatest marketing stuff. Brad likes to find shiny new squirrels. He may switch from one database to another database because the new database looks cool. He may have a perfectly fine buyer web lead system, but decides to switch to a newer buyer web lead system. Every single time a database or marketing system is changed or abandoned, Brad is losing tens of thousands of dollars but he does not know it.

No Clue Carol

No Clue Carol does not have a clue about her financials and net profit. Once a year, she panics and throws a pile of statements and receipts at her accountant. Her business may be doing great, growing fast, and be over $1,000,000 in GCI, but she wonders if she should be making more than her current $150,000 net profit per year.

Vivid Vicki Vision

We want all of you to have a Vivid Vicki vision. Vicki has vivid clarity about her business and financials. She does monthly financials and achieves a Billion Dollar Agent profit margin of better than 50 percent. In fact, Vicki often makes more net profit than teams that did two times as much sales volume and GCI.

What is My Net Profit Goal?

Based on your business size, here are the Billion Dollar Agent Profit Model numbers. Low means you have a problem. Medium means that you are doing okay, but it could be higher. Target-High is your ultimate goal. This is for a team which is $500,000 or more in GCI. The numbers may be higher or lower based on the average sales price.

	Low	Medium	Target-High
Net Profit	20-30%	40%	50%

If your net profit is 30 percent or lower, you should give us a call to see how we can help.

How do I do Monthly Accounting and Financials?

I firmly believe that businesses that do monthly financials make more profit than businesses that do not do monthly financials. Many small business entrepreneurs hate accounting. They hate the idea of having to do accounting or understanding accounting. They would like to just get out there, sell stuff, and close deals. I said it, the unspoken truth. Do not feel bad. If you are a top salesperson you likely dislike accounting. What do you hate more, accounting or databases? It is a tough call!

Over ten years, it will be worth $1,000,000 to improve your net profit from 20 to 30 percent or from 30 to 40 percent for a Billion Dollar Agent Business. Do you see the impact? It is worth facing the challenge of moving from a salesperson to a businessperson.

In speaking to hundreds of top agents, I can usually sense how much salesperson versus businessperson they are. The most powerful mix is someone who is a businessperson with excellent salesperson skills. If you are mainly a salesperson, your challenge is to learn what is needed to properly run a $1,000,000 business. The key is to focus on your unique talent and delegate everything else.

For accounting, we recommend that you use an online accounting system such as QuickBooks Online. You want to have three key people who have easy online access to your financials. You need to be able to access your accounting system remotely to view reports or check information. Your bookkeeper needs to do weekly and monthly data entry. They need to update information and run monthly financials. Your accountant needs accountant-level access to do your annual taxes and review quarterly financials to make sure the bookkeeper is doing everything correct.

For most teams, once organized, doing the monthly accounting only takes a few hours each month. Best Agent Business provides accounting services to get your QuickBooks organized. After that, we do the monthly bookkeeper steps. You should be able to hire someone for $15 to $30/hour to do a few hours every week or month. The monthly financials can then be sent to you, your accountant, and any advisors.

An important part of your accounting is getting your financials to match both reality and records. To do this, you will need a combination of coding for reconciliation of cash and checks, and other entries for business purposes.

If your Brokerage takes out your split or desk fees from commission checks before they come to you, you will need to add them back and state the proper total commission. You will need entries for each fee type. This is a huge problem and it causes confusion for agents at some of the top franchise brokerages. It gets more confusing depending on how they handle buyers' agent commissions. I have spoken to teams who thought they had $550,000 in GCI for the year and they really had $750,000 in GCI once we added back brokerage fees and agent splits. Their net profit margin was much lower than they thought.

Billion Dollar Agent Profit Model – The Secret Formula

Here is the secret formula to improving your net profit. We have organized this in the order of focus, depending on your situation.

- Marketing
- Agent Commissions
- Brokerage Fees
- Assistants
- General and Admin
- Revenue Extra

Marketing

- You should be spending ten percent on marketing. If you are spending 15 to 25 percent, you are likely spending too much.

- Stop wasting leads. What percentage of leads do you think you are wasting? Most teams spend too much on marketing and too little on calling. If you are spending 20 percent on marketing and wasting 50 percent of leads, that is a quick ten percent improvement in net profit to reduce marketing until you stop wasting leads.

- If you reduce marketing from 20 percent to ten percent to stop wasting leads, this improves your net profit by ten percent ASAP. That is a simple, huge jump.

- If you feel bad about getting fewer leads, remember that once you get your business balanced, you can increase marketing again.

- Marketing is often a five to ten percent improvement in net profit.

Agent Commissions

- The buyer's agent model is broken. It does not work for the majority of large teams.

- Best Agent Business invented the showing agent model in our first Billion Dollar Agent book in 2007. We have been testing and developing the model with a few top agents over the last few years.

- Many teams pay their buyers' agent a 50/50 split. If an average buyer deal takes 20 hours for $6,000 commission, the buyers' agent is making $150/hour to make that $3,000 commission. How many times have you given your buyers' agent a lead that is ready to go, such as referral or sign call you personally converted, they work for 20 hours and make $3,000?

- The showing agent model involves splitting the buyers' agent role into three roles of callers, showing agents, and closing assistants. You can hire unlimited callers or showing agents at $20/hour. Best Agent Business can call your backlogged leads or you can hire in-house callers. Showing agents paid $20/hour will end up costing about $500/deal including the 50 percent of buyer showings that fail to result in a closed sale. In a typical brokerage office of 100 agents, there are easily five to 20 agents who would be great as showing agents and happily work part-time for $20/hour. We provide more details on the showing agent model in another section of this book.

- Instead of paying $3,000 in agent commissions for a buyer deal, you may be paying out $500 to $1,000 for callers/showing agents. Instead of paying out 50 percent, you may be paying out 20 percent. This is a huge difference which has a positive impact of ten to 15 percent in net profit change for the overall business.

- Shifting from a buyer's agent model to a showing agent model for your buyer business can increase your net profit by a solid ten percent from 30 to 40 percent or 40 to 50 percent.

- As your business grows, you may start thinking of handing off some of the listing agent work from yourself to someone else. Do not do this too soon and do not overpay. Remember, you are making $1,000/hour or more on listing appointments. Running your business makes you $50/hour at best. You could hire someone more capable than yourself to be the chief operating officer at $50/hour which is $100,000/year. When you hire Best Agent Business, you actually get those services for even less.

- We have seen agents who make a terrible mistake and pay their agents a 50 percent commission on the listing side and 50 percent on the buyer side. You may as well run a brokerage and reduce your net profit to ten percent. That model is a disaster and you will end up with a brokerage, not a team.

- So what should you pay for a listing agent? Depending on the price range of your homes and the tasks you need done, we have seen people pay ten to 25 percent. That is too much. Everything that can be done by an assistant, should be done by an assistant. Some tasks are unlicensed and some are licensed. You can hire very experienced, part-time agents to help with listing assistant work such as gathering information, drafting a CMA, first walk-throughs, photos and details on the property. To get a more specific CMA, have them come with you on the listing appointment. Get them to stay and gather MLS details after you win the listing. If you paid someone 20 percent of the $6,000 commission or $1,200 for tasks which took ten hours, you would be paying $120/hour. This makes no sense. You can have that done for $20/hour or $200.

- A big mistake of agents over $1,000,000 in GCI is handing off listing agent work too soon, handing over too much, and overpaying the agent commission split. This will destroy your net profit. Real estate is a profitable business when done correctly. No one does $500,000 net profit on a $1,000,000 business. It all relates to making $1,000/hour or more on listing appointments. If you let yourself get burned out on listing appointments and you move from doing ten per week to one per week, your business will suffer. It is much better to pace yourself and keep doing three to five per week.

Brokerage Fees

We like to see five percent spent on brokerage fees, or $50,000 on $1,000,000 in GCI. If you are spending 15 percent, that is way too much. You need to consider brokerage fees and office space. Typical problems include the following:

- **Agents -** You should not be paying the brokerage fees, desk fees, or CAP of your buyer's agents. They should pay those themselves.

- **Office Space -** Having too much office space or paying extra for office space will be a fee above and beyond your brokerage fees.

Assistants

You should be spending ten percent on assistants.

General and Admin

You should be spending five percent on general and admin other than the above items. Remember, items like postage and printing should appear under marketing, not general.

Revenue Extra

Extra revenue usually comes from three main sources. These examples are all based on $1,000,000 in GCI:

- **Transaction Fees** - Almost all top teams charge buyer and seller transaction fees of $395 to $695 per deal, or more. If you have a $6,000 commission and get an average $500 transaction fee, that is more than an eight percent increase in profit margin.

- **Outbound Referrals** - If managed well, you can generate $10,000 to $50,000 per year in outbound referrals for sellers moving to other cities and incoming buyer web leads that need to get their home sold before moving to your city.

- **Vendor Marketing Money** - The largest brokerages and franchises focus on profits from RESPA-compliant mortgage and title business relationships.. If you are a Billion Dollar Agent, you should be getting five percent of revenue from co-marketing efforts with mortgage, title, and other vendors. For other vendors, we like to see one vendor a month pay for your monthly mailed newsletter.

With a combination of transaction fees, outbound referrals, and vendor marketing money, a Billion Dollar Agent may generate an additional $100,000 in revenue per year which is a ten percent increase in profit margin.

Summary – Growth or Profits

If you are at $100,000 to $200,000 in GCI, most of the previous material may not connect with you. You have not experienced going from yourself and an Assistant doing $200,000 to $400,000 to a team of five to ten people doing $1,000,000 in GCI. Your best bet is to share this with a top team and ask for their feedback on whether our analysis is correct.

If you are a future Billion Dollar Agent doing over $500,000 or a Billion Dollar Agent doing over $1,000,000, then it is likely that you are experiencing a variety of emotions after reading this analysis. You can now do one of the following:

- Ignore reality and be a **Big Ego Brad** or remain a **No Clue Carol**.
- Worry and Stress about your current reality.
- Become a Billion Dollar Agent by making a commitment to improve your net profit and call me to discuss how we can help.

Billion Dollar Agent Company Vision

Billion Dollar Agent Company (BDAC) is a public company valued at over $1B with over $1B in revenue and profit margins of 20 percent for $200,000,000 in profits in 2016. BDAC reached $1B in revenue faster than Microsoft, Amazon, and Google. Starting as a partnership consolidation of 100 plus Billion Dollar Agent Businesses (BDAB) in 2014, BDAC grew to over 500 BDAB in 2016.

Within the real estate industry, the top teams doing $1,000,000 in GCI revenue combined unique talent, systems, and the Billion Dollar Agent vision to move from an average of 20 percent profit margin to 40 percent and accelerate growth to a target 20 percent market share per BDAB. Starting as a book, *Billion Dollar Agent – Lessons Learned* in 2007, Phase 1 included research of 1,000 top teams and the creation of a beta test of the Best Agent Business support system of assistants and callers for 100 clients.

In 2013, Best Agent Business launched the *Billion Dollar Agent Manifesto*. Best Agent Business interviewed 1,000 agents above $1,000,000 in GCI to identify and select the best 100 to start BDAC. Over 10,000 top agents in the real estate industry read this 1,000 word vision during 2013. Of those, about 1,000 of them reached out to the author, Steve Kantor of Best Agent Business, to provide feedback, comments, and suggestions. Of those 1,000, there were about 100 who understood the power of the vision and started working consistently towards the creation of the Billion Dollar Agent Company.

The agents tested the concept by doing business with Best Agent Business and implementing Billion Dollar Agent systems to focus on their unique talent and improve their net profit. Many of the top coaches in the country agreed with the BDAC vision and became early investors. A core of ten Billion Dollar Agents invested in late 2013 as angel investors to build-out the platform to grow to 100 agents.

During 2014, systems expanded and BDABs grew from the initial ten to 100 with organized sharing of systems, unique talents, and platforms. The business and financial structure to combine businesses was defined and agreed upon. In 2015, the new business BDAC was created and ownership was rolled-up and combined. Growth continued in 2015 in terms of revenue growth and new BDABs to grow to 200 with average revenue of $2M. In 2016, BDAC grew to 300 with revenue of $3M and a run rate of $1B annual revenue as BDAC went public at the end of 2016.

Business Model – Billion Dollar Agent Company

BDAC is a new disruptive business model in the residential real estate industry based on creating a Billion Dollar Agent Business with an average of 50 deals per agent. The industry average is six deals per agent. RE/MAX skimmed the top cream of the industry to average 15 deals per agent during their 30 year record of fast growth, BDAC is designed to provide a growth plan and exit strategy for the top one in 1,000 agents in the country.

BDAC emerged from the opportunity of real estate teams becoming the fastest growing segment of the industry. Most of the teams are run by salespeople who are learning to be entrepreneurs and businesspeople as they grow a business from $100,000 to $1,000,000 revenue. However, 90 percent of teams have lower profit margins than what is possible. By sharing knowledge of business systems and profit maximization, BDAC increases the overall profit margins of all BDAC teams.

BDAC is not a new real estate franchise. It is not a competitor to RE/MAX, Coldwell Banker, Prudential, or Keller Williams. In fact, a BDAB can operate within a brokerage such as RE/MAX or Keller Williams or independently. BDAC is not a consumer brand; it is an elite option only available to selected Billion Dollar Agents over $1M in GCI.

Financial Benefits of BDAC:

- **Profits -** Increase net profit margin by 50 percent over three years by increasing net profit from 20 percent to 30 percent or from 30 percent to 45 percent as examples.

- **Growth -** Increase revenue faster by maximizing market share of current market segments and adding all possible Billion Dollar Agent market segments to every BDAB including client marketing, farm marketing, expired marketing, FSBO marketing, buyer open house, buyer web leads, vendor marketing, radio, custom newspapers, and more.

- **Taxes -** Increase after-tax income for hundreds of Billion Dollar Agents. BDAC will be structured with tax advantages and compensation structure to shift some profits from regular income to deferred capital gains.

Owner Benefits

- **Focus on Unique Talent -** Most owners are spread too thin and do not spend enough time on their unique talent. The BDAB owner can focus more time on their unique talent both working in their specific business and more importantly by working on specific market segments for all of BDAC. For example, the expired marketing or buyer open house experts could focus a few hours per week on building out and improving the systems for all of BDAC. The shared platform provides talent team support for assistants, callers, and showing agents for recruiting, hiring, firing, training, and managing.

- **Billion Dollar Agent Triangle -** The power of the system is the cooperative mastermind and sharing of ideas and accountability across 100 plus business owners. Instead of only interacting at periodic industry conferences for a few days per year, owners are organized into triangles of three and circles of nine with clear structure and accountability. By spending one focus hour per day on BDAC, the owner enjoys being able to work on their business with a system, structure, peer support, and accountability. Rather than spending 20 hours per year collaborating, they will be spending 200 hours per year.

- **Exit Strategy with True Liquidity -** Currently, almost none of the BDAB with $1,000,000 plus in GCI would be able to find a buyer for their business. By combining their company with BDAC, which grows to become a public company, the owner has true liquidity and finally has an exit strategy.

Overview of Billion Dollar Agent Business (BDAB)

A BDAB works using the business model from *Billion Dollar Agent Manifesto*. Staffing of assistants, callers, and showing agents are provided by a combination of Best Agent Business and staff hired directly by the owner. For a market with a $200,000 average sales price and $6,000 commission, a $1,000,000 in GCI business will have the owner act as the listing agent doing about 80 deals and showing agents doing about 80 deals. As the business grows, a listing assistant will be added and a buyer's agent to run the buyer consultations. The next growth level is 500 deals for $3M in GCI and then 1,000 deals for $6M in GCI or a 20 percent market share for the area, whichever comes first.

Agent and Coaches Interview Quotes

LONNIE BUSH

We want to plaster our name out there and gain recognition, we want to be the name people hear and instantly recognize.

Over the years I've had so many different Coaches in the business and they all tell you the same thing or a lot of the same things. We all know that's what we need to do, but we tend to go down our own paths. I think it's because most of us are successful and such independent thinkers that we have to do our own thing. A lot of times we have to go through our own failures to get to our successes.

When you start talking to everybody else about what you're doing – and you aren't doing it - it really makes you look at yourself. You look in the mirror and say everybody else has got something going on, I don't.

PAUL CHIOLO

I wish I would've scheduled myself better, sat with people at different times, understood where they were at and how I could help them. I wish I would have kept my pulse better on my team.

BOB CORCORAN

The markets have shifted so much over the last 23 years, especially over the last ten years. We've been through just about every imaginable market we could.

Top Agents mastermind quite a bit with other top Agents around the company. A lot of the major franchises do an excellent job of helping the Agents mastermind, but they don't teach them how to run a company. Agents are master sales people, but they are horrible managers.

RUBEN GARMYN

We're trying to get this going again and with the interest rates so low, it will keep going as long as we get enough inventory.

In my opinion, the industry is transitioning to mega-teams, teams with people that are really specialized in each facet of the Real Estate transaction.

COREY GEIB

Out-of-sight out-of-mind is true for a lot of people. When I find out a past Client did their Real Estate transaction without me, I have no one to blame but myself. I didn't follow-up and maintain the relationship that I should have.

We decided we didn't want to have someone else in control of our business. We need to be in control of our business. Whether it's the government or banks, I don't want either to be the majority of our business. I want it to be a segment of our business, but not a majority.

MARTI HAMPTON

We used to do a big, full-page spread in our local newspaper. At that point, in the mid-2000s, people were still looking in the paper. As time went by that became less prevalent. We moved our message to radio. Radio was one of the first things that gave us instant access to the people we focus on - home Sellers.

LAURA HARBISON

When I saw the market changing, I knew I had to change with it. The traditional equity sales almost disappeared. I had to redefine my entire staff, focus on what types of sales were going to be in the market place and put myself in a position where I could be ready for those.

I try to reevaluate every six months. I watch the market. I feel like my business should mirror the percentages that are in the market. For instance, if the market is 30 percent foreclosure listings, my inventory should be 30 percent foreclosure listings. The same is true with short sales. If it is 44 percent short sales, then I need 44 percent short sales. I've always kept that philosophy through the years, so I've been able to adapt and stay on top of my market for all these years. I watch trends and stay in place with that. My staff has gotten used to the idea that their jobs are going to change because they have to. At least they know they are still employed.

I am continually watching and listening to the forecasts the banks are giving. A lot of it is a common sense approach. What goes up must come down. Try to look ahead.

CHRIS HELLER

I was doing the business; I had my team, my Assistant and my staff. Then it became a WE – we're working together as a team. Now in 2013 it is THEY that are doing it. What I mean is because of hiring talented people, the right systems and putting the right people in the right places I've been able to step out of the business on a day-to-day basis and the business continues to grow.

The great thing is when you have a business that runs off systems that focuses on lead generation, it really doesn't matter what the market is doing. My business has never been impacted by whether it's a good market or a bad market. I don't even know what a good or bad market is because in every market there are people buying and selling homes.

PAT HIBAN

The logical and traditional way for Realtors to get business is through referrals and past Clients. The best Agents prospect to past Clients and ask for more referrals every day. This is a truism.

AMANDA HOWARD

I feel God puts things in your way for you to grow. He does it at the right time for you. I see people who get in the business and they talk to a bunch of people for advice. They jump into the seminars and classes. They learn, which is great, but they also learn all the excuses. They learn what's normal and what's not.

I have a vision for my company's growth which makes me happy. I also know we couldn't be where we are today if it wasn't for individual team members so I have a strong focus on the Agents and support team members in my company.

Pay attention to your people and know what's going on with their families, have one-on-one time.

DARREN JAMES

We're trying to take gratitude and magic and implement those into our business. It doesn't matter if our Agents sell a $100,000 home or a $5M home to a Client. It is important to that Client. It needs to be important to our Agents and our team. We try to create moments of magic throughout the process to show them they are important to us. You're the reason we're in business. Your transaction is much more than a transaction. It's a way of life. You had a choice. There are tons of Realtors in the area. There is one on almost every corner. They had a choice to choose us and we're very grateful. We try to go the extra mile and model it after Disney World and other businesses that give unbelievable service.

DAWN KRAUSE

I got into business with incredibly talented individuals. After they were trained, my business started moving to another level.

The most important thing in my mind is customer service. That is how I grew my business. I focused on my Clients. I didn't look at transactions as a paycheck. I looked at the people. When we focus on the people and what's in their best interest, the paychecks will come. Be purposeful and don't allow the outside stuff to let you lose sight of what's most important, the people!

Real Estate is a very emotional industry because of what people go through when they're buying, selling, etc. It's always been my number one priority to make sure that I'm focusing on the Client whether they're a $100,000 Client or a million dollar Client. I treat them the same. I taught my team to treat them the same. When we focus on that, the success of the team and the business comes as a by-product.

PATRICK LILLY

I believe that as I become a better human being, I become a better coach and Real Estate Broker. As I become a better Real Estate Broker, I become a better human being. The two are connected. It's all about learning, growth, education and experience.

CARLTON LUND

I've learned a lot, but the most important thing is to actually have an office with people I know will do a good, responsible job.

You've got to attract and retain groups of people you would be proud to have represent you or them. It is critical.

I have seen how the best do it. Whether you're in Real Estate or you're selling coffee, it is about customer service. It's about making it a worthwhile experience.

WES MADDEN

When times got tough and the market shifted, I started looking at my business from the perspective of a CEO. Maintaining profitability is my number one duty. If we're not profitable, what's the point of running a business?

We really focus on past Client referrals and Sphere of Influence referrals. We incentivize our licensed administrative staff to generate referrals to offset their salaries. That is all kept on a scoreboard in the administrative office so they can compete to see who can bring in the most referrals. It's fun. Everybody in the entire organization needs to understand that we can all generate referrals.

Agent and Coaches Interview Quotes

Appendix

Letter from the Editor – Jennifer Young

Six years ago I had a two year old daughter and a son on the way. I was worried about making ends meet, and was hoping that I could find a job that wouldn't interfere with family time. I scoured the newspaper, checked all of the online job sites, and purchased memberships to a number of work-at-home mom sites.

I found tons of minimum wage jobs. I found get-rich-quick scams at home craft jobs that paid a pittance. None of these were viable options. As a last resort I checked on Craigslist and ran across a very brief ad. The ad was for a position working with a new company. They wanted people willing to Kaizen. I have a degree in Japanese studies and I was interested to see who would want to Kaizen. I contacted the poster and quickly received a reply with an extensive list of questions about my likes, dislikes, and passions. I filled out the form and was quickly hired and offered a position.

During my time with Lifebushido and Best Agent Business I have worked in a variety of roles to include marketing, graphics, book editing, publishing, research, and writing. Through this whole time I have worked remotely from North Pole, AK. I have been very active, scaled back, took a hiatus, and returned based on my personal life. I have been able to change my tasks to suit my interests and available time.

Lifebushido and Best Agent Business have allowed me to put my personal life first, balance my time, and pursue my unique talents. These are three employment traits that very few companies have.

I am excited about what the future holds, I believe anything is possible and I look forward to seeing how Lifebushido and Best Agent Business expands to make even more people successful and happy.

Letter from the Editor – Raquel Martin

I am sitting in my office on a Friday afternoon, sipping a cup of coffee and completing a Letter to the editor for this book - *Billion Dollar Agent Manifesto.* This scenario has become a familiar one to me over the years.

It has been over 2,600 days since I coordinated my first project for Steve Kantor's Lifebushido. Yes, that was more than seven years ago. The project resulted in the world's first crowdsourced book – *YRUHRN? Why Are You Here Right Now?* It was an incredibly positive project. It cost a single penny to recruit me. I'm sure Steve would be happy to tell you that human resource story. Give him a call. I have had many phone meetings with my boss Steve, for many hours, for many years, but I have never met Steve in person. We live on opposite coasts of the United States. Our meetings are lively and I feel a great connection and sense of camaraderie when I speak to Steve. Steve always has crazy ideas. There is nothing I enjoy more than turning crazy ideas into concrete realities. I am organized. I am focused. I pay attention to details. I get work done. I am blue. Systems are blue. I love developing systems!

Lifebushido and Best Agent Business have brought me into contact with some of the greatest clients and team members I have ever had the pleasure of working with. This is a place where I have the autonomy to dream, create and innovate. This is a place where I know that anything is possible.

Appendix

Appendix